FALLING
AWAY
FROM ME

A Journey of Courage, Confidence,
and Character

DALE E. SIMILTON

Author headshot courtesy of Jeff Siner.

Cover and interior design by King's Daughter Publishing
www.KingsDaughterPublishing.com

Falling Away From Me: A Journey of Courage, Character and Conviction

ISBN 978-0-692-69670-5
Printed in the United States of America

DEDICATION

This book is dedicated to all those who follow in the footsteps of Jesus Christ, and those who walk by faith and not by sight. All of my life, I have known that God had special plans for me. Even as a child, I could feel God's holy presence within and around me. So, when it came time for me to write this book, I made a promise to God that I would share my miraculous story, because I believe that every one of us must bear his or her cross. I hope that after you have finished reading this book, your faith will be strengthened, your life's journey blessed, and most importantly, you will embrace the idea that each of us had to fall away from ourselves to embrace the life that Christ has ordained for us.

May the grace, power and love of the Lord be with you.

~ Dale E. Similton

ACKNOWLEDGEMENTS

My deepest gratitude goes to the following people who assisted me during my journey of developing Courage, Confidence, and Character. These are the true heroes who gave of themselves in a variety of ways. I will always be grateful for how they have blessed me.

The love of my life — my wife, Mildred
My sons, Joseph and Daniel
My family
Mrs. S. Kristi Douglas and King's Daughter Publishing
Dr. Ned Fox
Mrs. Diane Fiume
Miss Kim Garn
Mr. Lon G. Hawkins
The Joubert family
Mr. Jerry Kemper
The Kiwanis Club
Mr. Chris and Mrs. Margie Mathisen
Mrs. Linda Mackay
Ms. Inell Roberts
Mr. Jeff Siner
Mr. Tim Stump
Mr. Roger Weathers
Mrs. Terry Williams
Mr. Doug Youngblood
Last but not least, my family at Central Church Of God in Charlotte, North Carolina

TABLE OF CONTENTS

FOREWORD

Today is the first day of the rest of my life, and I would like to share it with you. May God bless your day! My name is Dale Similton. I love my divine assignment which you are about to read.

Let me begin by sharing a poem I wrote – one that carries the theme of my life, centered on the building of courage, confidence, and character in other people.

Dear Friend,
Oh, what do you say, when the people you care for go away?
And what can you do to show your gratitude,
So they may know that 'good-bye' is only the beginning of a new day?
First, we can count the times we spent laughing,
And caring for one another.
Second, we can let our love be all those words
That were never spoken in time past, and time to come.
And last, we can look toward heaven for guidance –
For our Savior is there, and it is He who has given us the opportunity
To experience this wonderful time we have shared
Yes, our love is the only way.

1

A Broken Childhood Built Courage

I NEVER GOT A CHANCE TO MEET MY OLDEST BROTHER, BECAUSE HE HAD BEEN STRUCK BY LIGHTNING ON THE FRONT PORCH OF OUR TINY SHACK BEFORE I WAS BORN. My other brothers told me of the tragedy years later. So I grew up for a long time in the little town of Kannapolis, North Carolina, assuming that my family had only ever been seven children. David was the oldest, then Greg, Janice, Ron, Wesley, me, and my youngest sister, Donna. And when I was about three or four years old, I realized that my family was poor.

My siblings gave me plenty of attention. It wasn't always positive attention, but for the most part, we got along quite well. Like many younger siblings in a family will do, Donna and I argued over almost anything we did together, because we fought for the spotlight. We wanted everything for ourselves, while in reality we possessed nothing of value. For her part, Donna was a kind soul and would allow me to have my way. Sometimes the others would step in and demand that I play fair, but I rarely listened to my siblings.

One thing was for sure: we all loved each other. We needed that more than other families, since our mom and dad were rarely at home. When they were, there was no peace between them, or in our house. Our father, Joe, and mother, Shirley, were rolling stones, never settling down. Mom got pregnant by Dad when she was no more than 16 or 17, and instead of having their first child out of wedlock, they got married. I don't really know how long their marriage lasted, but our lives were a nightmare from the time of our births to the time that social services discovered my siblings and me living alone and barely surviving. I called us "The Dirty Seven."

My older siblings played a vital role in demonstrating courage to me in my early years, especially David, who took the "father" role in our survival during childhood. He became a true champion and hero to me, as we lived on the brink of disaster in a world of drunks, poverty, sexual and verbal abuse, and shattered dreams. If I knew then that our security would come from just us, the Dirty Seven, I would never have believed we could make it to adulthood.

When we were growing up, our parents would come back to the house every so often to check on us. Sometimes Mom would bring strange men home to stay overnight, or for a few days. There was never enough money to get food to go around, so every day we struggled to survive. Sometimes neighbors would bring food, but on many nights we would go to bed hungry. I remember a time when I was so desperate for food that I ate any leftovers I could find in trash cans.

The little house we lived in had a tin roof, and when it rained, we had to put out containers to catch the rainwater. We all slept in the same room in one bed because there was no other space. The only source of heat we had during the winter was an old stove, which got so hot that it turned bright red and glowed like a star throughout the night. I really liked watching that star because it allowed me to feel some comfort and security, if only for a little while.

Our bathroom was an outhouse about 25 yards from the shack. It was filled with all types of spiders, and sometimes snakes would slide through to interrupt our train of thought. The snakes gave me a great deal of fear and anxiety about going to the outhouse, but my brothers accompanied me on my visits. The outhouse always had an awful smell, which even took over our living space.

There were many days I cried myself to sleep because I missed my parents. I guess all my siblings missed them, but we didn't talk about it because the pain of loneliness that we all felt was so great. David quickly emerged as our family leader and made every decision for us, because he knew we couldn't depend on Mom and Dad. There were no relatives that wanted to take on the extra load of our family, so we scraped by from day to day, living with hope and prayer. David impressed upon us to love each other, because it would be only our own strength to help us make it. He made sure that we continued to go to school, even when we had nothing clean to wear. David's primary concern was that we should not give up and be like our parents. He pushed us to grow up and show courage, confidence, and character in a world that had given us nothing but hell. One day, I realized that I survived only by the sacrifices made by my siblings to give me food and protection.

Violence was all around us. There were many times relatives would be fighting in the streets for everyone to see. Alcoholism was rampant in the different houses where we sometimes sought refuge. One day, our grandfather got drunk, chased me and some of my siblings with a water hose, and then beat us with it. In that moment, I felt my life being torn out of my body at every blow from that old madman. The terror and the beating may have lasted only minutes, but it left me with a nightmare that would not go away.

The biggest shock of my young life came on a cold winter night when I was almost six. I went to find warmth at the house of one of my sister's friends. There lived two older women who made bootleg liquor in the house and sold it to the neighborhood drunks. I was welcomed into an extremely dark and quiet house by a lady named Ms. Louise. She gave me food to eat and time to rest and get warm. For a short while, I felt safe in the cozy home. But suddenly, speaking in a hushed voice, she began to touch me in an area that I never experienced a touch before. This was shocking to me, because I never felt these sensations before. She forced herself on me, but I couldn't physically do what she wanted me to do, so she told me to go find her boyfriend, who lived down the street. Feeling guilt and shame, I went out into the cold and darkness, and time seemed frozen. I could never bring myself to tell my siblings about what happened because I didn't think they would have believed me. For many years, I tried to convince myself that it did not happen, but every time I would see this woman who had done this to me, I felt ashamed and could not bring myself to make eye contact with her.

One restless night as my siblings and I were gathered to sleep all in that one bed in our shack, there was a loud commotion at the front door. Mom had returned home. She never asked about how we were getting by, but acted as if everything was normal — as if she had always been with us. She brought in a tall, dark-skinned man who had the smell of beer on his clothes. But this woman had become a stranger to us, and I sensed that this surely was an evil man with her. Mom demanded that we return to our room and not bother them for a while. I knew what they would be doing in the room next to ours, because she had done this many times before with other men. David and Greg left the house because they didn't want to be around. The rest of us just held on to each other, hoping that the nightmare of Mom being there with that cruel man would pass. They were there for several days before the man even told us his name. To me, "Ted" was an evil man because he hated us for being there, and mistreated me, as if he knew one day I might reveal his dirty secrets. He physically and sexually abused my mother right in front of us, and physically and verbally abused my siblings.

One night in particular, I remember "Ted" coming home drunk and upset, over what I don't know. He blamed me for something, and threatened to beat me with his fists, as my mother watched without saying a word. But David stepped in and protected me from that man. To this day, I'm grateful to David for saving me that night. These kinds of episodes would take place often. It was not until my brothers got a little older that it stopped, because they threatened to retaliate. Finally, Mom and that evil man left and never returned. Once again my little family of siblings stood alone, but together.

David remained our fearless leader and continued to be there for us. We attended grammar school, which was a four-mile round-trip walk each day. Donna was in kindergarten, I was in the first grade, and my siblings were in second, third and fourth grades. I was not a nice child, nor was I a smart student. I can't recall if we ever did homework, because when we got home from school, we were mostly concerned with getting our next meal.

Finally, someone reported our situation to social services. They came to the aid of seven children who were in desperate need of love and attention. As I look back today, I have no doubt the only thing that allowed us to survive to that point was the courage God gave us.

Here's a poem I wrote concerning that time in my life.

CHILDREN OF DREAMS

Oh, so many tiny faces lie before me, and

behind me, but never beside me.

I cry desperately to bring them closer, because their little voices

remind me of memories that I've stored away for eternity.

Yes, they have the strength of the wind, and

the determination of a raging sea.

Still, I cry silently trying to bring them closer to me.

While their images fill the space around

me, so many eyes cover me.

From the darkness, I see the color of rainbows engulfing their

souls, as I cry compassionately for the ones that have gone.

Still, their voices come to me in my sleep, because

they never leave us in a world of misery.

It is their innocence that we seek, for

they are the Children of Dreams.

2

NEW BEGINNINGS
BUILT CONFIDENCE

THE DISCOVERY BY SOCIAL SERVICES OF THE DIRTY SEVEN WAS A NEW BE-
GINNING FOR ALL OF US, BUT WE WERE NOT SO SURE OF ITS VALUE. We
were placed into separate foster homes, because no one could
take seven kids at one time. We were gaining comfort, care and safety
— but losing our family. I was placed with my five brothers in the home
of a lady nicknamed "Big Mama." Her real name was Lola Neal. She
was already in her late fifties. She was a Christian, and she was strict.
David and Greg resented her discipline, because we had lived those
years before without any guidance, and both of them had developed a
strong independence. So the two of them decided to move out and live
with friends.

My sisters were each placed in a home with people that were loving. Donna was placed in a home in the same town as my brothers and me. Her foster mother was in her early forties and not married, but had lots of relatives staying nearby. Janice was placed in a home that was quite a distance from us. She lived with a couple in their late forties. Her foster father was pastor of a nearby church.

At that time, I didn't realize this separation would be permanent. Even as adults today, we've never been together as a family like we had been when we were children living on the edge of life.

My brothers and I grew strong and confident because of Big Mama's love and beliefs. I remember many spankings that I received from her, but I came to love her very much. I lacked self-discipline in many areas, which she corrected with a backhand or a good spanking. My brothers loved her too, because she went to extremes to meet our needs.

We stayed together with her for about four years. During that time, we saw Dad occasionally. He worked as a garbage man, and on certain days he would come to our neighborhood. We enjoyed seeing him, because he would give us money. It never crossed my mind to ask him why he didn't keep us, or where Mom might be living, or how she was doing. I don't know why I didn't ask. I guess it was too much for me at the time — as long as my siblings and I were safe and somewhat together, I felt content with my life.

Each summer morning was a new adventure for Ron, Wesley and me. Our back yard was filled with all types of wonderful creatures that my brothers and I loved to play with until lunchtime. We found a great place to pick blackberries for Big Mama, so she could fix our favorite dessert — blackberry pie. We were allowed to do some odd jobs in the neighborhood for pay, which taught us responsibility.

There were always chores around the house that needed to be done — including beds that had to be aired because we all wet the bed. Big Mama was not so understanding when it came to our bed-wetting. She thought we were too lazy to get up and go to the bathroom during the night. It took us a long time to overcome this problem, but Big Mama pushed us in the right direction with some stern discipline – and some embarrassment, since she made us hang our own sheets outside. But it taught us responsibility. Big Mama would say things like, "Act like you been somewhere," while she was telling us to behave ourselves.

Christmas was a difficult time, because Big Mama had little money to buy gifts for us. Many times we got nothing for Christmas, except for maybe a bag of candy. On Christmas morning, other kids would be riding their new bikes or playing with their new toys. We would hide inside the house until Big Mama made us go out and play. It was embarrassing to us when we had nothing new to show the other kids. We learned to accept the fact that we wouldn't be getting anything for Christmas, but it made us closer as a family and made us appreciate the true meaning of Christmas, which is the celebration of the birth of Christ.

We became better students during our stay with Big Mama because she gave us confidence. She helped us with homework, and made sure we completed it. She would wake us up early to make sure we did not miss the school bus. If we missed the bus we'd have to walk to school, because she didn't own a car, nor could she drive.

Ron and Wesley made great progress in school, but for a while, I reached a stage of total rebellion I don't completely understand. I was tired of living in my brothers' shadows at school and at home. I could never measure up to them, because they were smart and well-liked by everyone. But with the help of Big Mama, that rebellion quickly passed.

Somehow, I knew then that God had special plans for my life, because I could feel his presence within me. I began to focus on the activities that I knew and liked best, and they were church activities. My brothers and I became Christians, thanks to God's divine grace and the strong influence of Big Mama.

Jesus changed my self-image. The more I learned about Him, the more I developed dignity and security in my life. I had been a loser, but I learned that Jesus loved me for who I was, and loved me like no one else did – even when I was still a smelly little boy. There were many days at the young age of seven that I would lead a Bible study at the local church on Wednesday nights. This was unusual for a child, but everyone seemed to be moved by the words that I spoke.

I anxiously anticipated the day when I was going to be baptized. I believed it would allow me to feel more confident in myself, as I experienced more of knowing Christ through being immersed in the waters. When the time finally came, I waited patiently in line, dressed in a white robe and feeling like an angel. I was only a step away from being touched by the holy water. It was my turn to be immersed, but suddenly, an elderly deacon told me that I would have to wait until the next Sunday because they had run out of time! I was devastated! I watched others become forever changed and more like Christ, but my dream was unfulfilled. I cried as Big Mama tried to console me, and reassure me that my time would come.

The hurt I felt turned into anger toward the man that had told me "no" that day. In a cruel turn of events, that week he died in a house fire that was started by a gasoline heater. Somehow, I felt that it was my fault, because of the anger that I felt toward him. I never lost those feelings and never discussed them with anyone.

The next Sunday, I wasn't denied my right to experience this new part of my life that Christ had in store for me. The water was cold, and it seemed as if the preacher held me under for an extra long time. However, when I came up out of the water, I knew that I was forever changed.

Following is a poem I wrote that captures those moments.

THE POWER OF LOVE

I truly believe

If love were in the hearts of all people,

There would be no fear or need.

I know love can do the impossible.

Just look in the mirror at your own reflection:

The truth is before your eyes.

Love is a spirit that covers our faces and blesses the soul.

For love is the miracle of life,

And the world stands in need of a miracle.

3

CHANGES IN CHILDHOOD BUILT CHARACTER

URING THE NEXT COUPLE OF YEARS, MY SIBLINGS' LIVES WERE CHANG-
ING. My two oldest brothers got into trouble and were sent
to a training school for five years. Then Ron and Wesley
went to live at a place called Boys Town. It was a place for troubled
kids, and kids in need.

It was only Big Mama and me at home, but my brothers were on my
mind daily. There was no one to talk with who could understand what
I was going through emotionally and physically. I was searching for
my own identity. So, I prayed for a day to come that I would be with
my two brothers whom I truly depended on for guidance. Although
they visited occasionally, I was still crushed when they left. Other than

Big Mama, all I had known as a child was people coming in and out of my life. With my new found faith, I was learning that God would see me through, because He promised that He would never leave me nor forsake me.

Without my siblings, time seemed to go by slowly, but I kept busy with household chores and playing with my friends. Big Mama was watching my every step, as if she was afraid that I would fail, or get into trouble. One of her rules for me was to be home before dark each evening. I must have been late at least four days a week, and Big Mama's expression was not a pretty sight when she opened the door. I would receive a stern lecture on being late, then a good spanking to remind me that I shouldn't be late again. She would say, "This is going to hurt me more than it's going to hurt you — so be still!" But being still never crossed my mind. Instead, I would dance all over the place and yell like I was dying – which only made it worse.

In addition to getting those well-deserved spankings, I learned so much from Big Mama. She taught me how to pray and how to love all people even when they don't love you back. She gave me hope for the future and directions how to get there. But most importantly, she shaped my character for the man I would become – even though I couldn't see that at the time. Although I longed to be with my brothers, I knew it would be hard to say goodbye to her, as the one person I knew that loved me unconditionally.

I left on my tenth birthday. A social worker told me that it had been planned all along for me to go to Boys Town. She said there would be more structure. She reminded me that when I first came to Big Mama, she had me sleeping in a baby's crib, and now Big Mama was in her fifties. We had both grown older.

The thought of being with my two brothers made me happy, but I was sad at leaving the person who taught me everything I knew about life to that point. Big Mama would visit on holidays, which meant that she would still be a part of my life. But I wondered who would look after her when I was gone. Big Mama must have read my mind at that moment, because she said that God would look after her like He always had done. I learned an important lesson that day: love doesn't end just because someone goes away. Love has no end because it stays with you wherever you go.

Here's a poem I wrote and dedicate to Big Mama, who is currently rejoicing in Heaven with the Lord. God sent me to her so that I could learn what He had planned for my life. She prepared me for my life's journey of spreading the love of God to the children of the world.

DALE E. SIMILTON

A Mother's Love

Dear Mother,

Time after time I find myself thinking of all

those special moments we shared,

but I never told you during those times

how much you really meant to me.

So, today I will share with the world how much you mean to me.

When I was just a child with tears inside my

eyes, it was your tender kiss that dried them.

When I was confused about life, it was you who

opened the Bible and read me God's words.

And when I was lost and afraid, it was your words of love

that inspired me to free myself from those chains and be a man.

All that you have taught me over the years

has kept me humble and strong and focused on my purpose in life.

And, though I have grown of age, my love for you remains

In perfect balance with your every footstep

because in my eyes it was your love that changed my life.

I will always love you, Big Mama.

When I got to Boys Town, I was welcomed by many new faces. There was so much to see and do that first day, it was impossible for me to have done it all or to have seen it all, and still I tried. My brothers were in school, but they had been told of my coming.

I was given some time to explore the campus until my house parents in the Kiwanis Cottage were ready to talk with me. I was nervous. I was only ten years old, and my living cottage housed 11 other kids from ten to seventeen, with different backgrounds and personalities. But as I gazed out over the campus, I realized how right my brothers had been when they had told me about this place they called "heaven in the real world." It was spring, my favorite time of the year, and everything was green and full of life. I thanked God for delivering me from the hell that I experienced as a child, and leading me to this Promised Land. I felt like Moses standing over the land of Canaan, the land of milk and honey that I read about in the Bible. At that moment, I made a promise to God to follow Him no matter what the cost.

My house parents, Doug and Cookie, were a nice couple. They had worked at Boys Town for many years. They told me about fun things that the kids did on school nights and weekends. They explained the rules of the cottage and their expectations, which sounded like a lot to me, including the rule that every child must attend public school and get good grades in order to participate in campus activities.

The campus consisted of two cottages, the Kiwanis Cottage and JC

Cottage, an administration building, and a gym. There were horses in a barn, and a basketball court located right behind my cottage. I would be living in the cottage for the next nine years.

On my first day, I was given a room assignment and chores for the week. If I did them to satisfaction, I would receive an allowance of $1.75, which I could spend at a nearby shopping mall. I was excited about that, since Big Mama had never given me money for doing chores.

When the school bus finally arrived that first afternoon, I was so excited to see my brothers that I could hardly contain my emotions. As they got off the bus, I yelled their names out, just hoping they were as excited to see me as I was to see them. They ran over and gave me a warm hug. They told me about their wonderful experiences in their first year at Boys Town, which made me feel even more blessed to be sent there. We reminisced about Big Mama, and looked forward to the changes coming in our lives. We even prayed together, and gave thanks to God for putting us back together. We felt that all that was lost during our early years could not be compared to the good life ahead of us.

During dinner that first night, Doug introduced me to the rest of my cottage residents. They were Chris, Dennis, Ronnie, Steve, and two sets of brothers: Eric and John, and Tony and Kenny — who was the same age as me and would be my roommate. Doug told us that a typical weekday for all residents consisted of getting up at 5:30 a.m. or 6 a.m., depending on which school you attended. You were expected to do your assigned chores, including cleaning your room and making your bed. Eating breakfast was the last thing you did before catching the bus. We got back from school between 3:30 p.m. and 4 p.m. There was free time until dinner in the cottage at 6pm. After dinner clean-up, there was mandatory study hall for one hour, then the gym would be open until 9 p.m.

When we returned to the cottages, everyone was required to take a shower. For those in grammar school like myself, "lights out" time was 9:30 p.m., and later for the older boys. I tried to take it all in, but I knew that if I had any questions concerning any rules, I could talk with Doug or Cookie.

Instead of sleeping, I spent the first night talking with my room-mate, Kenny. He and his brother, Tony, had been sent to Boys Town after some relatives reported that their parents had been physically abusing them. Kenny resented being at Boys Town, because he felt that they didn't deserve to be put into a youth home, when their parents had created the trouble. We talked about our hopes and dreams. Kenny said the only dream he had was to be a racecar driver and felt, just maybe, his dream could still come true. I shared with Kenny my dream of becoming a pro football player. We finally decided that in order to dream, we'd have to sleep first, even though we didn't get much that night.

My first morning in the Kiwanis Cottage came with the sound of a voice that I would become familiar with over the years. The light would come on, as this easy but firm voice would say, "It's time to wake up and start a new day!" It was Doug's only wake up call. He would come by twice to see if I was up, but if he had to come by a third time, I received a small drenching of ice cold water on my face.

Doug took me to school the first day to enroll. My brothers had already told their teachers from the previous year that their little brother would be coming. Everyone thought highly of my brothers at home and at school. Although I hadn't been a good student in the past, I told myself that I had to excel, because my two brothers depended on me. I had a second chance to be a better student and demonstrate better character.

Before I left for school, I told my brothers I loved them. I saw Kenny off to the side, and he did not look happy. I yelled at everyone, "Look out for that racecar driver!" It brought a smile to his face.

In the school office, I was greeted by smiles from everyone. I never experienced this before, not even at my old school. I fell in love with school. The teachers showed me how much they cared for me as a student and a person. I had a burning desire to keep learning throughout the days of life. I was always compared to my brothers at school, but it was only a matter of time before I established my own identity.

The teacher who inspired me the most was my fifth grade teacher, Mrs. Gamble, who I still feel today had the heart of a saint. She was there during the worst experience I had at school.

One day, two famous pro basketball players visited our school. Mrs. Gamble invited us to bring in articles or pictures of ourselves to share with them. The men went from student to student, allowing each to share their moment of success. I waited with anticipation to show them a few pictures of me being a part of a team and in action playing basketball.

When they arrived at my desk, and I began to share with them my moment of success, I felt as if the whole world was listening as I stumbled through my little speech. But to my surprise I heard one of them say in a soft whisper to the other, "He will never amount to anything because he doesn't have what it takes." I was devastated that day, but I never shared it with anyone. Even now as I reflect on that event, I can still feel the hurt I felt as a child. I left all the tears I had on my pillow that night.

I moved on to junior high, sharing two years with Ron and Wesley before they moved on to senior high. We all participated in school sports — basketball, football and track. But we always focused on our grades, because we knew to reach our goals, good grades had to be our priority.

The person who inspired me most during junior high was a librarian who gave me my first job. I shelved books and kept the library clean and orderly. It was a turning point for me, because I was searching for my own identity and responsibility. I was tired of being compared to my brothers in the classroom and in sports. I looked forward to working in the library each day with Mrs. Roberts, who was a short black lady with an enchanting smile and a great sense of humor. Sometimes I wished she had been my mom. She believed not only in me, but in all the children around her. She was special to me, because she made me realize that it was okay to trust someone with my feelings, instead of hiding them inside, as I had done my entire childhood.

I continued to work in the library throughout junior high. Mrs. Roberts became my visiting resource at Boys Town, along with Big Mama. I now had two people in the world that cared for me. I remember my first weekend visit to Mrs. Roberts' home. I thought she was rich, because there was so much food. She had a back yard big enough to hold all the kids at Boys Town. Mr. Roberts was a gentle and kind man, who had a beard and a soft voice. He warmly welcomed me into their home, then hugged his wife and smiled. I had never met a great couple like this before.

Then I thought, "Why couldn't my family have turned out like this?" The only answer that came was an empty feeling inside. That weekend we did a lot of fun things together, just like the family I had dreamed about as a child. We attended a college football game, went swimming, and visited some of their friends. It was like a dream come true, until it was time for me to go back to Boys Town. On the way back, I began to count the stars in the night sky trying to block out those thoughts of home.

When I got back to Boys Town, like so many other times, I found myself longing to be a part of a family. I said goodbye to the Roberts' and stood waving until their car lights disappeared into the darkness. I felt numb all over as tears began to build inside of me like a swollen river searching for an outlet into the sea. I just couldn't allow the tears to overtake me. What would the other kids think?

So, I ran inside the Kiwanis Cottage, trying to leave what I felt outside in the darkness. I was greeted by Cookie, who asked about my first visit with the Roberts. I looked up to see if she really wanted to know, because no one ever asked about my feelings before. When I realized she was sincere, with a big smile, I laughed and shared with her my unforgettable weekend. That night before I went to bed, I thanked God for blessing me with special people like the Roberts and my house parents, because I knew they loved me.

But I didn't know why. How could anyone love someone who was never wanted before? That night, I could feel the hand of God reaching out to me and reassuring me that His love was forever.

4

HIGH SCHOOL DAYS

A S I MATURED INTO HIGH SCHOOL, I KNEW THAT NEW CHALLENGES
AWAITED ME. I knew that the Roberts family and my brothers
would be there for me, to support me, but I also knew there
would be situations I would have to face alone.

I made the junior varsity football team, which gave me a sense of
achievement. I worked hard so that my teammates would respect me
for who I was and not judge me for where I lived. I was doing well
academically, which came as a surprise. I was not a great student, just
a hard worker. I stayed up late many nights doing homework, because
that was the only time that I could study without being disturbed by
other kids playing around or making noise.

Ron and Wesley were great role models throughout my time in high school. Even though they were one year ahead of me, we were always close. Each of them lectured me many times about my future and their departure from Boys Town. I think they knew how much I needed them, even though I never said it to them aloud. No matter where I went, I felt their spirits with me. They were my guardian angels that shared in my miseries, joys, pains, and successes. This helped me to learn that God loves us even when we cannot love ourselves. His love is always steadfast and unchanging.

Wesley was successful both in the classroom and in sports through-out high school. I was so proud of him. He went on to attend a local college and studied physical education and played basketball. After he graduated, he joined the Army. He was a selfless person, who always put others' needs first. Ron excelled academically throughout high school, and he enjoyed popularity with the ladies. After he graduated, he joined the Air Force. At the time of this writing, both of my broth-ers are still serving in the armed forces. The saddest day of my life was when I said goodbye to them as they left Boys Town.

My last year of high school at Boys Town was filled with excitement and disappointment. One fall night, I was on the football field, with that sound of screaming voices and a certain chill in the air. I felt like a true warrior, wearing my helmet and armor. I waited to do battle on a field covered by numbers and lines, and the field lights reflected our shadows, making them larger than life. This was Friday night football as I remembered it. But one particular night, my life would be changed forever. During the game, I received a kick to my thigh, which I had previously injured my senior year. I was able to run off the field under my own strength, but as the game wore on, my thigh yielded to the pain inside. I had never experienced pain like that before, and I felt helpless and scared. We won the game, but I felt like I did nothing to help the team, and I felt I was losing my dreams.

My thigh got worse. I tried to push myself in practice to show my teammates – who had admired my skills — I could still play. And I wanted to let the coach know that I was not faking the injury, which he suspected, and had accused so many other players throughout the years. He did not respond with empathy, but with an attitude of disbelief and verbal bitterness.

I was in disbelief myself. Just a few days before, I was healthy, and he and the other coaches were confident in my abilities and supportive. As my abilities had failed me for whatever reason, God allowed me to see the true nature of this man whom I called coach. I decided then to never put my trust in man ever again, but I would look toward God for guidance and understanding, because I learned that His love never changes. From that day forward, I knew that no matter how bad things might seem, God would not allow evil to overtake me.

On doctor's orders, I quit playing football. He said that if I did not rest my thigh for at least five to six weeks, I had a good chance of becoming crippled. My team continued to win without me, and eventually won the first state championship for their division. But I believed that God, in His perfect timing, would one day give me an opportunity to win a championship.

In the months ahead, I had to endure personal attacks on my character and on my desire to be a team player. Even my relatives questioned why I had quit the team. This made me question my decision, but I remembered what Ron had told me before he left to go to the Air Force: always believe in yourself and continue to move forward, even when everyone else doubts you. I continued to display a positive attitude in school toward my coaches and peers. At Boys Town, I was considered a leader and positive role model for the other kids just like my brothers had been for me. My cottage parents were instrumental in getting me to focus on attending college, which helped me to put more emphasis on my future instead of the past.

My thigh finally healed and I was able to play basketball. I was excited because I had missed playing football, and I had a chance to play for a coach who was a Christian. He had taken special interest in my brothers and me, which was not due to our skills, but because he wanted to see us make it in life and to be good people. I saw in him what I wanted to see in myself — a man of character. He was a godly man who accepted people for who they were. He would give us rides home after practice and games, and would give us lectures and guidance on life.

It was a wonderful basketball season. I learned a lot about winning with humanity and losing graciously. Although we did not win a championship, I won something more valuable — a love for the game of life and being a positive role model. My basketball coach set a standard that I thought every coach, including myself, should aspire to reach.

The following is an article that God inspired me to write, which was published in a local newspaper in November 1994. It shows how important it is for adults to lead by example, because there are children waiting to follow.

For four years I have been teaching and coaching at Charlotte Latin School. My day long involvement with children has given me an opportunity to observe and attempt to meet their complicated needs. I wish to share some thoughts about children and their future, which is our future. My experience has made me realize that adults, whatever their relationship to children, need to be more than just role models. We need to carefully guide them down the road to tomorrow. To do this job, we need to be parents, teachers, preachers, and disciplinarians. As we guide them, we should remember to do so in a way that keeps their dreams alive, because they follow in our footsteps. They are so impressionable, so yearning for acceptance, so fragile. Every word we say creates images in their minds and affects their dreams. Therefore, we should beware of how we speak. Their nature is one of peace. Oh, and they love without reason, because their trust is from the heart. That's why before they rest we should hug them with all our might, to assure them that it is good to be loved and to show love and that love is a path to change the world. For tomorrow, children will inherit this world. Our footsteps on the sands will no longer be visible.

Our job will have been done, and the images formed in the eyes of the child never grow old.

("Guide kids, but keep their dreams alive." Reprinted with permission from The Charlotte Observer.)

5

TIME OF CHANGE

I WAS TURNING EIGHTEEN, WITH ONLY A FEW MONTHS BEFORE GRADUATION. I was nervous about my future, because the security of Boys Town and the world that it had created for me would be gone. Although my counselor kept me focused, I was afraid of taking that same journey that my brothers had taken before me. I lost myself in a relationship with a beautiful young lady who was also about to graduate.

I had dated her off and on throughout high school. She was my first love, and I was hers. I believed that if her heart would ever stop, mine would, too. If I could not be with her, then my purpose for living would be without meaning. If she would ever leave me to go far away, how would I ever learn to love again? I was madly in love with this girl, who also had dreams and a destiny which I thought may somehow coincide with mine.

It seemed that every good thing concerning my life to that point was coming to an end. Time with my brothers, my joyous days at Boys Town, shoe-less carefree childhood days – all were coming to an end. I had become wise and learned of the boundaries of this world. As for my shoes, I've learned one must travel the road of life, not with just one pair of shoes but two, because time and directions change.

WHAT DOES GOODBYE MEAN?

So, here we are for the last time

Face-to-face as our emotions run high,

As we wait for someone to say goodbye.

So, what does goodbye mean, when I know that

tomorrow I will still be in love with you?

For the love we created is so beautiful, while

those times we have shared are unforgettable.

So, what does goodbye mean, when I know that

tomorrow I will still be in love with you?

I'll just touch you, and you hold me, and

time will be ours once again.

Because our hearts will be free like the

hour that we first fell in love.

So, what does goodbye mean, when I know that

tomorrow I will still be in love with you?

I loved you then, and I love you more now. And

I will continue to love you throughout time.

So, what does goodbye mean, when I know that

tomorrow I will still be in love with you?

I will always love you.

6

COLLEGE DAYS

URING THE JOURNEY TO MARS HILL COLLEGE OUTSIDE OF ASHE-
VILLE, NORTH CAROLINA, I BEGAN TO REALIZE THAT THE OPPORTU-
NITY OF A LIFETIME AWAITED ME. It was a beautiful winter day
with the chill of frost in the air. As the wind danced in circles and the
trees swayed, my thoughts ran free. I found myself looking through
a window of life, trying to imagine what college life would be like. So
many images filled my vision, as thoughts of playing football before
thousands of cheering people left my soul thirsting for more. A smile
touched my face as thoughts of falling in love with someone that I
never knew but desired to share a moment in time seized my heart.
Haunting those thoughts, I felt an anxiety that caused me to wonder if

I was meant for college or if I was born to walk a path of failure, never to feel the spirit of success. I could not believe God had brought me this far to leave me, nor allow my dreams to be unfulfilled, because I knew He had called me to be a leader of men.

I was excited about playing football during my first year at Mars Hill. I enjoyed making new friendships. I stuck to my Christian values. I was more determined to succeed than ever before in the classroom and in athletics due to my negative experience in high school football. Still, I trusted God to guide me.

Although my first experience with college football was a bittersweet one, I learned from every experience. The sweetness came on my first play during a game. I was playing wide receiver and the coach allowed me to run a reverse from my receiving position. The play turned into a 49-yard touchdown run, which set my football career into motion. The bitterness came that same season when the head coach was fired during one of the early games. I didn't know the reason for his termination but all hell broke loose. The players protested. We were the first college football team ever to go on strike during a season, which made national news.

I was upset concerning the whole situation, because I came to play football and not get involved in turmoil. Eventually, I had to make some crucial decisions regarding the stand that I would take, either to support the strikers or play football with a team that would be plagued with negativity throughout the season. The team captains called many meetings, but to no avail, because there was no team unity. Eventually, an interim head coach was put in place to finish the season. He issued an ultimatum to the players: either play or lose your scholarship for the season. I was no longer interested in taking sides; I just wanted to do what I was expected to do. A deadline was set for players to return if they wanted to finish the season. I missed the deadline because I was late getting to the meeting with the other players and the new coach.

It was a sad time for me, because all I ever wanted to do was to get an education and play the sport I loved. It was over for that year, and I lost my scholarship. I also lost my ability to trust in coaches. I anticipated going back the next season. For the rest of that first year, I was able to take out loans to cover the cost of school. I resented having to take out the loans, because I felt I was at the wrong place at the wrong time. But I continued to do well in academics and fell in love with the beauty and peacefulness of the mountains.

I was wiser in my second year. The academic year went well, and my friendship grew with a guy named Bernard Steadman, who had survived the strike and helped me adjust in my first year. Bernard was about 6'3" and weighed about 240 pounds. He was from Blacksburg, South Carolina, and along with being a nice person, was the funniest person that I had ever encountered. I believe he was a Christian, but not always acting like one. Nonetheless, he respected my faith walk. Many times, he and I traveled the road to Charlotte, North Carolina together in his big green Chevrolet. He lived with his grandmother, who had raised him and placed the fear of God in his heart. He talked about her often, and I had the chance to meet her on one of our trips. She truly believed in God. She reminded me of Big Mama, which brought tears to my eyes.

The football season was going well, because God allowed me to begin exactly where I had left off. I scored five touchdowns in two games, and was playing well on the special teams. Then, in the fourth game of the season, tragedy struck again. On my first play of the game, returning a punt, I fell to an injury which I felt was done deliberately. In the midst of a pile of tacklers, I was at the bottom with my adrenaline flowing. I could not feel any pain, but I could hear and see someone from the opposing team step on my ankle. When I got to my feet and tried to jog off of the field, I took two steps toward the sideline and the pain suddenly set in. From there I had to be carried off the field. I felt cheated, sitting on the sideline, unable to help my teammates or myself. The thought of someone deliberately hurting me was devastating to my will to compete, because everything I had learned about sportsmanship was being tested again.

I had a fractured ankle, which would take at least six weeks for healing and then rehabilitation. I was in shock leaving the doctor's office. How could God allow this to happen, when I was giving Him the praise and glory for everything that had taken place concerning football and my life? I decided on my way back to campus with a cast on my right ankle, to face this obstacle with determination and faith, knowing that God would cause me to rise again, to be even better than I could imagine. I decided not to harbor any bitterness toward that player who caused the break, but would forgive that person in my heart. I had realized long ago that forgiveness allowed me to find true peace from within my soul, and to establish character.

About that time, I fell in love with a pretty mountain girl. She cared about me as a person, not whether I was able to play football or not. I truly felt that God placed her in my life for a reason, and I received her gratefully. Throughout the rest of that year, my life became more interesting, because I was in love. Still, in my heart I longed to be on the football field. Every chance I got, I would attend practices and games.

At the start of my junior year, I was ready for whatever challenges that would come my way. My ankle rehabilitation went well, and I was in love. I thought this football season would be different because I told myself I would pray before each game and work harder in practice. I would not waste a moment of the time God gave me to play the game I loved. Even though we had a new coach, I refused to allow that to hinder my positive thinking about the season.

In the first couple of games, I was struggling to work through the psychological part of being back from the injury that I had sustained a year before. There were some frightening moments throughout the season, but with God's help and with the support of my girlfriend, I made it through. I finished the season being named second team all-conference receiver. I was third in punt returns and fourth in kick-off returns, and led the team in yardage per catch. These were more than just miracles to me; this was God's way of letting me know that He had chosen me to be a leader, if only I would believe.

The academic year also went extremely well. I changed my major from religion to psychology, because I believed that God wanted me to work with people in a different capacity. My girlfriend graduated and went to work in another town in North Carolina. I knew if our love was truly meant to be, distance would not be an obstacle.

When my senior year arrived, I was anticipating setting the football world on fire because God had allowed me to train throughout the entire summer. I was bigger, faster, and more determined to take our team to the top of the conference. Again, we had another new coach. We had a new transfer quarterback who came in the spring of my junior year, showing great promise. Bernard was in the best shape of his football career, ready to block, and always ready to make me laugh any chance he got. My girlfriend had promised she would return to see me play and be my cheerleader.

The football season was spectacular, and the academic year was even better. Our team was nationally ranked, and I was leading the district and conference in touchdowns and reception yardage. When the season was over, we had accomplished the impossible: the Sac-8 Championship belonged to Mars Hill. I was interviewed by my hometown paper about the possibility of being drafted by the NFL. I was named Honorable Mention to the Small Colleges American Team. I had broken several scoring records and led the team in scoring throughout the entire season. All of those memories of the hurt and pain I had experienced throughout my athletic career from high school through college were gone, because a champion had been born out of courage, confidence, and character. I celebrated with my teammates and I thanked my coaches, and I told my girlfriend how much I loved her.

The journey had not been an easy one. It took prayer, dedication, determination, unity, and faith to conquer the mountain which I had faced throughout the time I had spent at Mars Hill. I learned through it all to never give up or give in to the pressures of life. And most importantly, I learned again to trust God and not man because God allowed me to see and do the impossible, through Christ working within me.

My college years flew by in a blur, and now it was time for me to prepare for the real world. I was nervous about a possible future in the NFL, but I decided on my way to the podium during graduation that God had the ultimate plan for me. I enjoyed that glorious day along with the many wonderful people who came to support and show their appreciation for this young man who had learned to climb mountains no matter how high they seemed. My next poem captures those golden moments that I experienced and speaks of the treasures that were given to me through love.

RUNNING

When will you come running?

If only summer was to come again,

We could live among the flowers and taste the honey of the bees.

The forest would be ever so green, with the small

animals stirring about, and living out their dreams.

When will you come running?

If only dawn would never fade, then there would be time

for us to play like children do in the school yards in May.

Soon, night will come creeping this way, as it always does.

Oh and day will go its way until she changes into something new.

So, do you not dare walk on steps made of

glass, when the earth shakes in anger,

Or do you freeze like an icicle does in the silence of winter?

For the heart of a lion doesn't come easy,

to those whose fear is their ghost.

When will you come running? Today or tomorrow?

For, if tomorrow then, I will forbid sleep, like

angels do, when expecting some glorious event.

I will not close either eye just in case you come by in white.

And those dreams will not be missed.

Like thoughts they will come again...

7

LIFE AFTER COLLEGE

WHEN I RETURNED TO CHARLOTTE AFTER GRADUATION, I WENT TO LIVE WITH DOUG, WHO HAD INFLUENCED ME THROUGHOUT MY ADOLESCENCE AT BOYS TOWN. He let me stay with him on the condition that within a year, I would either be playing pro football or working somewhere in Charlotte. I was honored that he trusted me with the keys to his house and car. I appreciated his friendship, because at that point in my life I was waiting, and living on a dream that seemed to be a million miles away.

One night Doug asked if I would be interested in working as a substitute counselor at the home for children which was formerly Boys Town. In my mind, all I could think about was preparing myself for the open camp tryout in Atlanta, since I had not gotten drafted, and this could be my opportunity of a lifetime. I was faced with a dilemma: either go work and train in-between, or continue to train. I decided to do both so I could have an income. I would be working in my field of study, and I could save money to buy a car. Most importantly, I would be able to go back to the place that had played such a big role in my lifetime.

I worked at the children's home for more than two years in the Kiwanis Cottage where I had lived. It was not an easy job, but I became better at understanding the needs of children. I became less self-centered, and more attuned to serving all humanity. During my time there, I understood the anguish that each child carried inside his soul but could not express. I shared in their triumphs, hopes, and dreams. Often, I would think to myself: if only God would hear their cries, surely He would save these children. Then I realized that God had heard their cries — and sent me along with others to attend to their needs.

I found I was no longer consumed with being a pro football player. I wanted more than ever to be in the footsteps of Jesus, who had brought me to this place where I met with my calling in life. Even though I did attend an open football camp in Atlanta and was mentally and physically prepared to show my talents, it was not meant to be. I came away, not defeated, but assured that God had called me to work with children in some capacity. I continued to work at the children's home several more months before God opened another door of opportunity.

I wrote the following poem for the children, which I read to them on my day of departure.

LOVE YOURSELF

Please, remember to love yourself, as you travel on your journey.

For it's not who you were yesterday that will lead you,

But who you are today, that will lead you to your destination.

Each day try and move closer to your dreams,

because they will only become reality

If only you believe.

In time your hands and feet will no longer

Be like those of children, but of men and women.

And then God will be your only source of refuge.

So learn to love yourself, and the love inside of your heart

Will sparkle like a diamond throughout time.

For you are special, and there's no one in this world like you.

8

ANOTHER DOOR OF OPPORTUNITY

AJOB OPENED FOR ME AT A BUSINESS COLLEGE, WHICH I TOOK WITH SOME APPREHENSION. In my spirit, I could not feel God's assurance that this was the right direction to take, but I still went anyway. Six months into the job I was let go, due to the fact that my recruiting was not consistent with the college's goals. I took this as a sign from God that it was not part of His plan for me to be there. I moved on without any hesitation, but this time I began to seek God more because somehow I had misinterpreted His will for me and I felt a deep regret.

I experienced many trials during the next several months. I never gave up on God, but in my soul I thought I had been disobedient and these challenges were His way of dealing with my sins. I worked two part-time jobs to make ends meet, and neither offered medical insurance. I got sick, and it seemed as if I would never get well again. I prayed daily and fasted on certain days, hoping God would show me mercy. I would cry and dream of times when life had been good. I still kept my faith, believing that God had chosen me for a mission work for Him.

My conscience did not let me forget sins that I had committed against God. I had been disobedient and not kept my body holy. I had not waited on God concerning my engagement, because He had a special person for me, but not the woman that I had chosen. I broke off the relationship with her because I knew God had been displeased with our actions and lifestyle. That hurt me deeply because I felt very alone. I kept faith in believing that God had forgiven me.

One night I fell asleep, and God showed me a premonition of the mission and place that He had planned for me. It was a place marked by beauty and adorned with peace. It immediately reminded me of Mars Hill, a place that I treasured. In this dream, the person who was showing me around was always a step behind and I could never see his face. It was so real to me that when I woke I felt revived and filled with the spirit. That morning I made three vows to God. Wherever He would bless me to work, it would be built around him. Wherever He wanted me to live, it would be His place of refuge. Whatever money He would bless me to earn, I would tithe so I would never lack again.

As I worked my part-time jobs, I had a sense of peace, joy, and confidence in believing that God would reveal this plan when everything was ready. I was no longer sick because God had healed my body and blessed me to be stronger than ever before. I worked with a new spirit, like I had when I walked with God earlier in my life. Even my thoughts were made pure because of my repentance to God.

One morning, I was working at a local YMCA, checking in members. A man came in, and his face seemed to be riddled with pain. I smiled and asked him if he was okay. He said his leg bothered him on cloudy days due to arthritis. I told him that happiness comes from within from God, and we should not allow outside events, situations, or weather to dictate how we feel. He just smiled and said he would try to remember those words.

A couple of months after that encounter, the director of the YMCA invited me out to lunch to talk about my future. He told me the headmaster at a local private school was interested in me as a teacher. My heart was on fire, and my spirit danced circles around the room because somehow I knew this was God revealing His plan.

The following day I called Dr. Fox at Charlotte Latin. An interview was set for the same day, which I was ecstatic about, because God was moving on my behalf. At my first interview with Dr. Fox, I realized he was the individual I spoke with at the YMCA about his arthritis. He took me on a tour of the school and introduced me to the faculty as a new teacher and coach who might be joining the staff. As we were walking up a flight of steps, and he was talking about the history of the school, he stretched his hand out in front of me showing and directing, but I could not see his face. I realized in my spirit it was the dream I had several months prior, and this was the place that God had prepared for me to do His good works. I remembered each vow that I had made before God the morning after the dream, which I was determined to keep.

I had two interviews in other departments which would be set up in the days ahead. Just as I had fasted and prayed before my first interview, I did the same for the next two. Finally I was selected to teach Social Studies and coach JV football at Charlotte Latin. There would be other duties that I would learn about later during the course of my career at Charlotte Latin. I was assured by God that this was the place where He called me and He prepared in advance by building up my courage, confidence, and character.

My first couple of years at Latin were a time of learning my role as a coach and teacher. I learned a lot, and established a positive relationship with the students, parents and faculty. In addition to being JV football coach, I was also appointed assistant varsity basketball coach. I kept reminding myself of the promise that God had shared with me many times before — that through Christ all things are made possible and that He was still forging my courage, confidence, and character so that I might become more like Him.

Before my arrival at Latin, the JV football team had a record of 0-6. With God's help, over the next five seasons the team gradually improved to a 7-0 record. This happened only by the grace of Jesus, because my last season was the most difficult one in my career.

Prior to the start of practice that season, I was told that I would receive limited help because there were not enough coaches to help. But I remembered that all good things work out for those who love the Lord.

During a Friday afternoon practice before our first game, a player received a blow to the head and was sent to the hospital. After going home, he passed out, and had to be rushed back to the emergency room. He needed brain surgery to stop internal bleeding. I didn't find out until Monday what happened, and I was devastated by the news. I went to see him that morning with a prayer on my lips and tears streaming from my eyes, not knowing how his family would receive me. Over the four days following surgery, the student recovered his ability to walk and other motor functions. The doctor said it was a miracle that he had recovered so quickly after having brain surgery. He returned home only a few days after I had visited him at the hospital. I gave thanks and praise to God for intervening in this situation and turning it to work out for His glory. The rest of the team decided to dedicate the entire season to this young man who would never again play football. The team supported him and loved him, and I was very grateful for that.

The season opener was an indication of what was to follow — we won that game 32-0, and then went on to beat a team which I had never beaten since being hired as the JV football coach. Varsity coaches reminded me many times that it would take a miracle to beat this one particular team. It's the game that I will remember for the rest of my life. Both teams came in with undefeated records that season, but our opponent had not lost a game in six years, which made our 13-8 win even more of a miracle and a very emotional win.

I wrote the following poem in August 1992 to those young men on that team and their families. I hope they still remember that it is not in winning that victory is gained, nor in losing can one be blamed. But in the struggle, your courage, confidence, and character is being shaped into a true champion for Christ.

IMPOSSIBLE DREAMS

I awoke last night inside of a dream

Where the impossible was made possible

By the faith of children.

So, I counted the children who stood

Like Greek gods with their shields of

armor shining like radiant light.

They were few in number, but their greatness could not be denied!

Even their size was small, but their minds

were purified by the wisdom of time.

For I heard them say, Our destiny is not a dream, if we believe!

While, in their eyes I could see only the

beginning of what was to be!

Yes, the impossible made possible by children

who believed in themselves and their dreams.

9

FALLING IN LOVE

I HAD BEEN PRAYING AND FASTING FOR A LONG TIME, ASKING GOD TO SEND SOMEONE TO SHARE MY LIFE. I was 31, waiting on God to answer my prayers. It was through one of my Christian students that God revealed my future wife to me.

There was a new student named Jane Logan in the Ancient History class I taught at Charlotte Latin. I met her parents on the first day of school. I felt comfortable talking to them, and they invited me to a service at the church that they pastored. I had intended to go sooner or later, but there was always someone or something that would come up to prevent me from attending.

One day I was doing car-pool duty after school, helping to keep traffic moving, and keeping an eye out to be sure the kids were safe. Mrs. Logan was waiting in the car pool line for Jane to arrive. I asked Mrs. Logan about single women at her church. She said that a lady named Mildred would be perfect for me because of our shared interest in serving God and loving children. I asked if she would have Mildred call me, because I wanted to meet her — but if she was involved with someone else at this time I would pass. I was willing to wait on God to fulfill my request for a special person in my life.

Months passed, and I did not hear the name Mildred again until the beginning of spring when Mrs. Logan reminded me of her again. I had thought Mildred was not interested, because she had not called me earlier. I asked Mrs. Logan to tell Mildred that if she would like to call me that night, I would still like to speak with her. I got home about 8 p.m. as usual, coming into my dark and quiet apartment, never thinking about the phone call that I had talked about earlier that day. The first thing I always did after I got settled in was to go to my bedroom, kneel beside my bed and share a special moment with God. I would read a Bible verse to acknowledge Him and to praise His Holy name.

Then, I checked my phone messages. There were two, including one from Mildred. What a surprise that was! Her voice was soft like the voice of an angel and her good-bye was like a harp playing with no end. So, I prayed that God would give me the words to say to this new person. I felt that, just listening to her voice, somehow she would have an everlasting impact on my life. I finally called her back an hour later, taking time to build up my courage. As I nervously dialed her number,

I felt like a little boy infatuated with a girl he's never seen before, only in his dreams.

On the third ring, that angelic voice answered. We had a light conversation telling each other about ourselves. Some would think my life is boring, I told her, because I'm simple. But most importantly, I told her, I love serving the Lord and other people because I feel that's what God intended for me to do.

She replied that she, too, was a simple person, and loved serving the Lord and others. I said, "Well, Mildred I hope we can be friends, since we share so much in common. What do you think?" She replied yes, but that she was very busy. Mildred was a professor at Pfeiffer University as well as attending and working on a Ph.D. in psychology at NC State. We decided to keep in touch by phone until our schedules allowed us to meet.

We talked on the phone for many weeks before our first brief meeting. But every time we talked, I thought she could possibly be the one that God had intended to be my wife. I knew in time that God would show me an answer if I would just be patient and wait on Him.

Finally, we set a time to meet during spring break. Even though it was only a week away, all I could think about was meeting Mildred. The plan was for me to drive up to the college campus, about 30 minutes away, and meet her in the afternoon. As much as I looked forward to seeing a face to put with the lovely voice, I could not imagine what Mildred would look like. On the drive to meet her, I could only think of what I would say to this person who had captured my heart over the phone. I realized that God would give me the words.

I arrived on Pfeiffer University's campus with the confidence that no matter what happened I would be happy just to have met this person whom I adored from our first phone conversation. As I parked the car, I reached for my Bible to thank God for getting me there safely, and to ask Him to speak through me that day to everyone I would come in contact with so they could be forever blessed.

I followed the directions Mildred gave me to get to her office. When I entered the building, several people greeted me, and I was shown to her office. There, suddenly, I was face-to-face with a person I thought was Mildred. So I politely extended my hand and said, "Hello I'm Dale, and it's my pleasure meeting you, Mildred!" But to my surprise, that person was someone named Tonya. She explained that Mildred was at a meeting and would be back shortly.

I waited for about twenty minutes before she arrived. As she came into the room, time stood still inside my mind. My eyes spoke to my heart telling it to be still and wait its turn! She said, "Hello. My name is Mildred!" as she placed her small hand inside mind. She apologized for being late, but in my heart I knew time would never be an issue for me, because I was willing to wait forever just to meet her.

We walked around campus most of the day. Mildred shared with me her visions for her students. I listened as she told me she really felt she was making a difference in lives of the people that she met. "Being a Christian," she said, "I feel and believe that God lives through me to reach other people. I know that I have a long way to go to be the best that God wants me to be, but I'll get there."

She stopped to talk to a student, and I waited for what seemed like forever. My only thoughts were thanking God for allowing me to meet this woman who walks in the ways of love.

"So, my life is nearly totally consumed with meeting the needs of other people," she told me a little while later. "I have little time for myself." That became evident in the midst of our conversation when another student walked by, and she stopped to talk to him.

As I waited this time, thoughts of love crossed my mind. The sun touched my face with a soft kiss allowing the moment to be captured forever inside my mind. When they finished talking, I asked Mildred if she would like take a ride in the country, because I knew it would be difficult to finish our conversation on campus. To my surprise she said yes, but she needed to be back within the hour. As we walked to the car a cool summer breeze seemed to whisper into my ear that love between us could be possible.

During our drive through the country we talked about our lives, the most important topic being how God changed both our lives. I noticed her unforgettable smile that told me of the joy that was inside of her soul. Time flew by. As I drove her back to the campus, I felt peace inside. I had experienced seeing a reflection of my love for life in someone else. I knew our relationship would not end there, and I believed she knew that it was only the beginning of what could possibly last a lifetime. She said, "Call me anytime, because I will be waiting. And I enjoyed the time that we shared today."

10

FAMILY EMERGENCY

O N WEDNESDAY, MARCH 22, 1995, AT ABOUT 8 P.M., I FELT A STRONG SURGE GO THROUGH MY SPIRIT AS I WAS TALKING TO MILDRED, MAKING PLANS FOR THE WEEKEND AHEAD. Suddenly, I was frozen in the middle of the conversation, as my body went through an emotional high, to a cold and downward spiral. I had experienced the feeling before, at a funeral many years ago. My body wanted to free itself from these feelings, but my mind seemed to be taken by a force greater than its own. I tried several times to stay on conversation with Mildred, but all I could say was that someone in my family was either in pain or needed medical attention.

Suddenly, I began to speak in the Spirit concerning my Father in heaven sending a warning of what was to be and I had to accept it, without even knowing it. I began to pray as the Holy Spirit covered me like a mother holding her firstborn. Mildred prayed in silence because I could hear her soft whispers. We finished praying but I was still troubled. I knew somehow that I would have to endure a trial.

On Friday, March 31, at about 10 p.m., I talked to Mildred again. I was still feeling apprehensive about a trial coming into my life. We talked until about 11:30 p.m., planning to meet the afternoon of the next day.

A few hours later, at 1:45 a.m., the ringing phone almost woke me from sleep. I was content to allow the answering machine to pick up. But a stranger's voice brought me more awake. I stared at the clock numbly to see if maybe it had an answer as to why this stranger's voice suddenly started making me cry like a child. I wanted to reach out through the darkness to cling to my mother. I was not ready for what was taking place. In my spirit, I could see a woman who lay dying in a hospital room with only moments left to live. Family members gathered in her room wondering if she would last another hour. The pain of losing her is far too great to bear, so they send up their prayers to heaven. I can hear their prayers as if I'm right there in the same room with them.

My tears wouldn't allow me to move. I cried silently, trying to ease the helplessness that I felt as the darkness hid my overwhelming pain. I sat up in bed and became a part of the darkness. In my mind, I tried to save a child who never developed a relationship with his mother, but had to learn to depend upon God and himself. In my mind, a child called loudly to his mother, as he stood there with tears in his eyes: "I love you very much, no matter what you have done, I still love you."

Suddenly, the strength of ten men filled my tired body. I turned on the light, and saw that same child across the room, staring at me. I thought to myself, this child needs me, but as I reached out to hold his hands, they become my own. I realized I was looking at my own reflection in the large mirror at the foot of my bed, and that child was me. I held on to what I believe in every hour of need: I looked to Jesus to give this man and child strength to endure what was taking place.

I played the recorded message back and felt loss that I never felt before or since: "Dale, please call the emergency room at Cabarrus Hospital as soon as possible, and ask for the nurse in the intensive care unit." I fell on my knees and cried out to God, knowing that only He could give me what I needed to make it through the hours and days ahead.

Mrs. Shirley Similton had internal bleeding and was in a coma-like state. There was fluid around her lungs, which may cause her to stop breathing. The doctors needed to know: do you want us to resuscitate her if she loses consciousness, or should we let her pass on? As I was talking to them, I would see my childhood flash before me again and again.

My heart cried out for someone who never truly was a mother. She left seven children to search for security and direction for themselves. Did she not catch a glimpse of any spirit in our faces when she held each one of us in her arms? Why did she not count the cost of each one of us, as we lay in her womb? With tears continuing to run down my face, I realized what was causing me to feel this way: I never once told my mother that I loved her. And I don't remember her telling me that she loved me. Now she was dying, not knowing the love that she's leaving behind, and never shared. It moved me to whisper a silent prayer asking God to restore all of the love that she lost her lifetime, and to let her know that, in love, there exists the power of forgiveness.

I talked on the phone with my sister Donna, and she was going through the same feelings: "I'm just afraid of losing her, because there are so many things I needed to tell her that I may never get chance to say." My mother died in a matter of hours after that conversation.

The funeral was held at a church that Mom had attended when she was a little girl. There were people there who knew her throughout her life. One lady who was blind said that Shirley did know the Lord, because she had been a mentor to her at a local church. Somehow, she had gone astray for whatever reasons. "Shirley was a good person at heart, who faced the world with no fear, but with a sense of adventure," she said. "At some point she got lost and could not seem to see her way back to the path."

There were no words that I could express to my sister to ease the pain, so I said nothing. But in the silence I knew that God was speaking to us. Once again, my siblings all held on to each other, realizing that what we had lost was far more than what we had all experienced as children. On that day, we laid to rest a lady whose past haunted her, but whose children learned to live better despite the life she gave them. I found myself just hoping that God would be there to answer my mother's call, because surely we all need His mercy.

Here is a poem that relates my ideas of life and death. To live is Christ, and to die is gain. I hope as you read this, you will develop a greater respect for life and a better understanding of death.

THE PERFECT WORLD

I have a dream of a world without color and no rulers. Every day is called joy, and there is a light that shines forever upon my face. I have wings like angels as I too fly to the perfect place. I feel so cold in this wretched place, but the streets of gold keep my feet from getting cold. I have a dream of a world with no time, as peace and love walk side by side, as I touch the wings of the dove that watches over me.

I feel so cold in this wretched place, but the streets of gold keep my eyes upon my goal.

I have a dream of a world filled by the sound of children's voices as their faces are covered by a holiness not seen by the eyes but only felt in one's soul. In the distance there is a sweet lullaby being sung by a Mother who's found her lost child.

I feel so cold in this wretched place, but the streets of gold keep my heart filled with faith.

I have a dream of a world that lives forever inside the eternal light, and the people there are pure in heart and known only by the love they have inside. I have a dream by and by, for I believe that my life has purpose, and my dreams cry out to those souls that I see when I'm awake, because they walk leaving no trace of where they've been. I can see no footprints in the sands of time but only their dying dreams, falling helplessly to the floor of the earth as the sound of a shovel full of dirt covers the face of another who's lost his dream.

11

LIFE AFTER DEATH

MILDRED WAS SUPPORTIVE DURING THIS PAINFUL, CONFUSING TIME IN MY LIFE. It was during this time that God revealed that she was the one that He had sent for me to marry and to cherish for my lifetime.

But I questioned the choice, because she freely disclosed some things about her past. She had been married before, and had only been divorced about a year and a half. She admitted to having made a mistake in marrying a man that her family never liked. She was not a Christian when she married or divorced, but during the suffering, she found Christ.

However, I had made a decision earlier in my life never to be a part of someone else's confusion. So why did God send this woman to me when He knew my expectations? I thought I needed more answers from God, because at the time, my needs outweighed all that I could see.

One morning, I prayed that He would confirm this was the person that He had prepared for me by showing me a visible sign on that day. It rained hard most of the day, and the streets were heavy with water. It occurred to me that maybe this was the sign that God was giving to me about Mildred, but my spirit wasn't moved.

Even as I went about my day, I was watching for a sign from God. When the rain stopped and the sun came out, I thought to myself, could this be the sign that I've been waiting for? But my spirit was not moved.

Suddenly, I saw a double rainbow. I had never seen a double rainbow before! It was then my spirit was moved, because I knew this was the sign that only God could have sent. I felt the presence of God smiling down on me, reassuring me that those who wait on the Lord shall be blessed.

Here is a poem I wrote about the miracle concerning someone who has been blessed with a wife from God. I find myself each night looking at my wife as she sleeps wondering, why me? But every good gift comes from the Lord.

RAINBOW

Dear Friend,

There's a rainbow inside my life that I prayed for day and night. It covers me wherever I go and comforts me in times of need. Although I've never seen it before, I know it's there because I walk by faith and not by sight. So, if you cannot see my rainbow just try and visualize love dancing circles inside your most perfect dream. While Angels sing a sweet melody that causes one's soul to leap for eternity. O Lord, thank you for my rainbow - for I never knew how beautiful life could be in the midst of storms and raging winds. I see daily what You have given me, which is more than I deserve but what You have desired for me.

Sincerely,

Your Humble Servant

12

WEDDING BY FAITH

I PROPOSED TO MILDRED BECAUSE GOD CONFIRMED TO ME THAT WAS WHAT HE WANTED US TO DO. We prepared for a wedding without any financial assurance, without any consent from her mother, with my bills unpaid. The only thing we had was our faith in God, knowing that He would provide everything we needed for our marriage and lives. It was February when we met, and in the same year on December 17, 1995, we were married. There were miracles that led up to the blessed matrimony.

Each day, I found myself longing for answers and expecting miracles knowing that God could do what He said would do. In my life, God has always been there to do the impossible, and I believed that He would continue, because it was His will for us to share our lives together. As I look back, it was never easy, nor did I expect it to have been. Throughout our engagement, so many things had to happen in order for our lives to work out together.

Mildred was moving from Pfeiffer University, where she had worked for five years, back to Charlotte. Then in just a matter of months she would leave to attend North Carolina State University as a full-time student. She did not know where she would be living in Raleigh. I was feeling emotionally unstable thinking about being married to a woman in another city whom I would see only three days a week. This was not at all the way I wanted to start our marriage.

In the meantime, Mildred's mother voiced her opposition to our marriage. She felt that Mildred needed more time to finish her graduate studies. She felt strongly about Mildred waiting to get remarried, since it had only been a little more than a year since her divorce.

We had no money to pay for a wedding, reception, or honeymoon. My school teacher's salary was not much, but enough to cover my cost of living. I didn't have any savings, and my credit was lousy.

I needed more than just one miracle; I needed God to stand in for me, as I became overwhelmed by all the obligations and problems that would either serve to strengthen my courage, confidence, and character, or cause me to doubt the awesome power of God. Many nights I would fall asleep thinking about how wonderful it would be if I were to wake up rich and carefree. Then I could marry Mildred with no worries. I knew in my heart of hearts that God had other plans for me. All of my life it had been in my struggles that God had revealed His omnipotent power either to deliver or restore me, and this situation would be no different.

During the months ahead miracles began. A family that I babysat for on many occasions offered to have a pre-wedding party for us. This beautiful family had a beautiful, palatial home that would be like having the party at a castle. We were remarkably blessed with generous gifts and kindness, and the party was attended by many friends. Truly it was an unforgettable evening, which was only the start of the miracles to come.

Here is the poem that God inspired me to write days later concerning the experience of that joyous occasion.

RESTORATION

On this day God has restored all that I once lost in time gone by. Even the children's voices sound like Angels singing a sweet melody that causes me to cry like a child. I feel love and I see love all around which makes my soul wonder how I could have ever doubted God's intentions for my life. Though a thousand thoughts cross my mind as I look out at all of the festivities going on around me, my heart focuses on what God is doing with me. Many trials and tribulations have I faced as child and as a man, knowing that only God would see me through. For somewhere in his plans included this time for us to meet, which today has been brought to fruition. So, as I stand on threshold of life, I know that I must finish God's plan for me, because it's in the doing that I will find peace, not in the knowing.

So, all that I do and say will be done in love, because my heart has been touched by God. As this special day comes to a close, I find myself where I started the day — on my knees thanking God for sending me to people who will honor his most Holy name.

13

MORE WEDDING BLESSINGS

ANOTHER PARTY WAS THROWN FOR US THE MONTH BEFORE THE WEDDING, AND I WAS AGAIN IN AWE OF GOD'S POWER AND THE MIRACLES THAT WERE BEING WORKED RIGHT BEFORE MY EYES. This party was also given by a family from Charlotte Latin which I had spent much time with and grown close to.

Their daughter, Amy, was on the varsity girls' basketball team, and I had counseled her and other players after some tough losses. According to her family, Amy treasured those moments and thought that I was one of the nicest people that she had ever met. I have felt honored over the years that she and other students have thought so highly of me, but at times I wondered what I did to deserve such compliments.

On that November night, Amy's family would celebrate with me some of the most precious moments that Mildred and I would treasure for a lifetime. As the evening unfolded, I understood how Cinderella must have felt thinking that somehow time would be interrupted and my dream would come to an end. Suddenly, thoughts of my friendship with this family consumed my total being, while the darkness outside stood frozen in time as the celebration continued inside with love shining through our souls and allowing us to be free. I desire to always remember what this felt like.

This particular poem concerns those relationships that have caused my soul to forgive and learn to live again.

A Child Inside

On the day I was born I felt so cold inside, as

I came into a world much colder than I.

My mother gave me a name but never gave me

love, and my Father denied me the right to be his

son. Still he said I looked so much like him.

Now I realize that images are made from lies. Meanwhile,

my soul cried out to know the truth, which I've found in

Jesus Christ. Today, I realize that it was a blessing in

disguise to be born in a world much colder than I.

Now, God is using my mind, body, and soul to coach and

teach His children about His eternal love and forgiveness.

Therefore, I can forgive a mother and father who left a child

with only a name, because my life has been forever changed by

relationships based on this New Thing that God is doing in my soul.

14

PARADISE IN DECEMBER

MILDRED AND I WERE MARRIED ON DECEMBER 17, 1995, AT 4 P.M., AND MY LIFE CHANGED FOREVER. She was, and is, my most precious gift and the joy of my life.

I shared that day with some special people, in the wedding party as well as guests. Most were people I knew from Charlotte Latin. Some of the students were honorary attendees, which captured my heart, as I looked out over the audience to see people whose friendships I treasured and lives I valued. This was truly a miracle to see a multitude of people of different races coming together to celebrate my most joyous day.

It was a reflection of how God had allowed me to live a life of loving others and walk in empathy concerning their needs. This was more than just a wedding; it was paradise in December. I'm sure angels were there, sharing in my glorious moments through which God was bringing into fruition the dreams and hopes of a child who once was abandoned, never felt loved, and who carried in his heart those secrets of a past life that scarred his soul. It was the new courage, confidence, and character which had been established through Jesus Christ that had changed my world.

On this day, I felt the very presence of God, just like I had felt during those times growing up in that dirty little old shack in Kannapolis with a leaking roof. This time I knew that God had blessed me with an inheritance, and all of what I was experiencing was just a small part of what He has planned for our lives. I could hear the bridal processional music echoing throughout the walls of my tender heart. The song was "Order My Steps in Your Word," which was fitting for the occasion. As the song played, I watched Mildred's every step, from her entering the church to arriving by my side. For a moment, my thoughts went back to our first meeting on the campus at Pfeiffer University where I fell in love with her beauty and elegance. I was marrying the person whose spirit I desire to cover me whether I'm awake or asleep.

This is a song I wrote which captures that very moment which God allowed me to be united with my soul mate forever. I hope when you are finished that it brings refreshing thoughts of that special day that either you fell in love with, or married that special person. My desire is to always remember, because it helps me to keep looking forward to where we are going.

BY MY SIDE

Oh, I kept my faith through my trials and tribulations when love was only a thought in my heart. And I denied my touch to more than just one stranger, because in times like these you need someone to trust, someone to hold when the world gets too rough, and someone to love who means so much.

So, here you are by my side loving me every day and night. And I always want you to be by my side, because my sun only rises inside your eyes.

Some people search all their lives for a place they call paradise. I found everything inside of you, because you give me reason to believe in love, where my heart is secure.

So, here you are by my side loving me every day and night. And I always want you to be by my side, because my sun only rises inside your eyes.

Oh, you changed my life — you have made me whole and now traveling down a brand new road loving a woman who watches over me whether I'm awake or fast asleep.

So, here you are by my side loving me every day and night. And I always want you to be by my side, because my sun only rises inside your eyes.

There's no better time to tell you this, I'm in love with you, and I want to be with you, and I want to spend my forever loving you.

And, there's no better time for you to be near me, as the darkness comes and covers me. I need to feel your love watching over me whether I'm awake or fast asleep.

15

MIRACLE YEARS AND SUMMERS

IN THE BEGINNING OF THE 1996-97 SCHOOL YEAR, I NEEDED ANOTHER PART-TIME JOB SO THAT MILDRED COULD CONTINUE WORKING ON HER DOCTORATE. God answered my prayer by October.

The director of the middle school where I worked approached me about working as a part-time youth director at her church. Mildred was thrilled about the offer, and we prayed and waited on God to confirm this divine appointment. A couple of weeks later, the head of the middle school approached me again, this time setting an interview with some people at her church. After prayer and fasting, I took the job. I was able to see many miracles in the lives of the youth at St. Francis United Methodist Church.

The following is an article that I published in a local paper concerning working with children with low self-esteem. Hopefully, after reading this article you will become more aware of how to better meet the needs of children.

In our communities today, there are all types of problems that we attempt to solve through various communications skills, which have been acquired through years of experience. Yes, adolescents struggle within themselves to combat low self-esteem with little communication skills. It is noted that low self-esteem causes negative behavior and enables the adolescent to acquire identities that would be acceptable to the outside world but not allowing them to love self.

As adults, do we care about their struggle? Ultimately, their struggle will become our problems as they enter into young adulthood. Maybe, one cannot conceive this to be true. Just observe your local news or read the newspaper for a small sample of the negative behavior of adolescents who are dealing with low self-esteem. How will you respond when it's your own adolescent struggling with low self-esteem? Will it be to give him or her more "things" or to reprimand without understanding, or will you simply accept this behavior as apart of today's norm?

As loving and caring parents you would be wise to seek the cooperation of significant people in your adolescent's life. Teachers, school counselors, parents, and adolescents should work together to improve low self-esteem. Hopefully, the adolescent will become empowered to channel his energies toward being positive and a productive citizen. Perhaps there are other remedies that can cure adolescents' low self-esteem. It is this author's opinion that caring people will always be needed to assist, for miracles are always worked through people who have a genuine love for humanity. Hopefully, this article will serve to enlighten people of the negativity that low self-esteem can perpetuate in adolescents who are in desperate need of courage, confidence, and character.

("Adolescents with Low Self-Esteem: Do We Care?" Reprinted with permission from The Charlotte Observer.)

16

KEYNOTE SPEAKER

NOVEMBER 19, 1996, HELD A SPECIAL EVENING FOR MY WIFE AND ME. I had accepted an invitation from the president of Elon Homes for Children to be the keynote speaker at an event that would be held at their campus in Burlington. This particular evening would celebrate the academic achievements of their students, as well as honor staff. A lifetime award was also set to be given, and new board members would be recognized (I had recently accepted an invitation to join the Board of Visitors).

I stood in front of a large audience of strangers who listened with their hearts and were changed by the message of love that God gave me to share on that wonderful night. Afterward, I remember the tears in their eyes and the joy on their faces when they, too, had realized that we are all interconnected through our courage, confidence, and character.

In June 1997, I worked at the Hornets Youth Basketball camp where I was chosen as Coach of the Year, honored by other coaches and Hornet staff. Mildred and I were blessed with the opportunity to work at a camp for our own church that summer, with good pay, and a good opportunity to work with kids. This wasn't our first opportunity to run our own basketball camp, which was something I always wanted to do. Over the years, our basketball camps have steadily grown in numbers. God has given us many opportunities like this. I truly believe God will bless us with our hearts' desires if we are obedient to His will concerning our lives.

Another miracle that happened that summer was that Mildred would be going back to work in July. It had been almost two years since she had been working, but during that time God had provided for us abundantly. She would also be working as an assistant director of a new camp established at Pfeiffer University, where she would be returning. She had asked me during my school year if I would be interested in facilitating an intramural program for this new program, called Quest. I said yes, because I enjoyed working with her. Also, it gave me another chance to work with adolescents who needed more motivation, education, love and guidance.

The week at the Quest camp changed my life, and reinforced my understanding that God loves children, and He desires for each of us to humble ourselves before Him, like children.

Here is an article that I wrote concerning those wonderful moments that I will treasure forever.

Today, I believe in miracles, and I believe that working together can make a difference. I came as an outsider to assist my wife in a newly developed program at Pfeiffer University known as Quest. The purpose of the program is to motivate and stimulate the bodies, minds, and spirits of rising ninth graders considered to be potential first generation college students. They were selected by the surrounding schools to be the first Quest participants.

During orientation, I had the opportunity to engage in building a relationship with many of the students' families which I enjoyed. Although the adolescents were nervous and filled with anxiety, I could see the excitement in their eyes concerning their new quest for success. So, as the intramural instructor, I engaged the staff and students in Play Fest. After several icebreakers and silly activities, the staff began to establish a trusting relationship with the kids, while they were bonding with each other in the areas of trust, commonalities, and respect. This set the norm for the entire camp.

Throughout each day, I noticed the instructors sharing their life experiences with the kids. I feel this served a major purpose — to assure a good working relationship between them. Also, I believe that it gave each young person an opportunity to share and to feel a sense of belonging and understanding. By the end of the day, I felt a sense of community forming among this group of adolescents who began as strangers.

I believe all of the learning and experiences each received will serve as a positive force to further develop their potential. This is truly the beginning of something special concerning the lives of this Alpha class of Quest. The staff has shared the vision of Quest, which has been well received by the group itself.

Finally, I know that each adolescent that participated this week leaves with a better understanding concerning work ethic, friendship, self, and the value of community. This is why I believe in miracles and working together can make a difference.

("Working Together We Can Make A Difference," Reprinted with permission from The Charlotte Observer.)

17

RAISING TWO GODLY SONS

I MADE A VOW TO GOD TO HONOR HIM BY GIVING MY CHILDREN BIBLI-
CAL NAMES BEFORE THEY WERE BORN. Through prayer, my wife and
I picked out the names Joseph and Daniel. The name Joseph
always was on my mind because that was my father's name. However,
Daniel appealed to me because the story of Daniel in the lion's den was
such a fascinating story to me.

Joseph and Daniel were born two years apart. My wife and I felt the
timing was good for their overall learning and development. I reminded myself daily that I never wanted to be an absentee father who did
not respond to the needs of his children.

Even before my children were born, I tried my best through prayer, dedication, and walking in truth with my neighbors to love much. God made it clear in His word in Luke 7, "if I love much, then much will be forgiven." I wanted this for my boys because it has served me well. Therefore, I read from the Bible and pray with my boys believing that God will sooner or later show them His purpose for their lives, just as He revealed my purpose.

It was a pleasant time for me during those early years in my boys' lives, as I would juggle coaching and fatherhood. The most challenging time was when I would go to play basketball on Saturday mornings. I would take my two little boys to the gym so I could play some basketball with my friends. While I played, I would put the boys in a holding crib so they could play with their toys. This never worked very well, so I had to either quit playing and tend to their needs or take them home.

Mildred gave me strict orders before I would leave the house: have fun, but make sure you pay attention to your boys. I made sure that I did, because I wanted to be a good father outside of my home. I knew that I could be a good father, and that I would have to make sacrifices in areas of my time, money, and future. I relied heavily on encouragement from the scripture in Philippians 4:13: "I can do all things through Christ who strengthens me." We dedicated both of our boys at our church in Charlotte. This was a "new thing" that God was doing in my life, and I could feel His presence in my children, marriage, and home.

Later, when my boys were older, they were baptized at the same church, and committed themselves to the cross of Christ. I'm proud to say both of my boys accepted Christ at a young age. My wife and I spent countless hours helping them understand that the love of God is unconditional and His mercy is forever. I even shared with them the stories behind their biblical names.

My dream for my two boys was for them to attend Charlotte Latin School where I had worked for six years before I got married. Joseph was the first to attend, while Daniel was still in preschool. Daniel attended later, and I was delighted. Joseph struggled at times with his writing motor skills, for which we had to seek professional help. During these times, I found myself questioning God and asking Him why He allowed my son to have these issues. He would simply remind me to read 2 Corinthians 12:9, "My strength is sufficient in your weakness."

After some time, I made a career decision through prayer, faith, and discussing it with my family. I believed it was time for me to make a career move to become a varsity boys' basketball coach at a Christian school. I got the job at Covenant Day School in Matthews, North Carolina. This would be a defining moment, because it would be the first time my children would attend a Christian school. For me it was a great leap of faith leaving 15 years of security to attempt a career in coaching on the varsity level.

During the transition, I checked on Joseph and Daniel every day. We would have long talks in the morning on the way to school about their likes and dislikes. The last thing we would do before we would leave each other on the campus was to pray together. I really felt that

God was my source and refuge during the year I worked at Covenant Day. I watched my children develop their learning skills and their physical capabilities.

My boys were settling down and building positive relationships with their teachers and peers at Covenant Day, but God provided another opportunity as the athletic director at Lake Park Academy, where my wife had worked for more than six years. This was a Christian school, it was in our neighborhood, and our own church had just purchased the school. My heart was torn for my boys because I did not want to see them move schools again, but I spent time in prayer with my family, and invited friends to help us pray to make the right decision.

God had been reinforcing the idea in my spirit that He would do a "new thing" in my life when I went to work at Covenant Day School. The verse is in Isaiah 43:18: "Forget the former things, and do not think about the past. See I will do a new thing..." I believed that God was about to do a "new thing" with my family, by sending me to Lake Park Academy (renamed Central Academy at Lake Park).

As of this writing, my boys have a stronger faith in God, and positive relationships with their teachers and peers. God has given me the opportunity to work alongside my wife and to live in a neighborhood where I teach and coach. We have lived here for 15 years now.

However, we experienced a traumatic trial with my son Daniel in 2012. He was diagnosed with a condition that required a heart procedure at Duke Children's Hospital. He fully recovered to play point guard for the basketball team. He is an excellent student and loves bible trivia.

Joseph is in high school, doing well in his studies and has his eyes on a basketball scholarship. He loves the Lord and spends a lot of time doing service work for others and making time for his passion, which is reading.

I pray with my sons each night, and after each prayer we recite together Philippians 4:8: "Finally brothers, I will dwell on that which is true, honest, pure, and lovely; if anything is of virtue, praise worthy, or of a good report. Whatever you have heard or seen in me, please do. And may the peace of God be with you."

18

MIDDLE SCHOOL RETREAT

ONE OF THE GREATEST SPIRITUAL MOMENTS OF MY CAREER TOOK PLACE AT A MIDDLE SCHOOL RETREAT WITH CENTRAL ACADEMY. My wife had planned the retreat for spiritual team building and establishing positive group dynamics. There would be ropes courses, field games, and swim time for the students. I was a cabin counselor with 8th grade boys during the retreat. Most of the eighth grade basketball players, along with my son Joseph, were in my cabin.

During our first night, the students were so excited about the day's activities that we spent time talking about every event. Later, I was able to share a little about how God wanted to help each one of them to achieve their dreams. I shared with them that I was a prime example of

God taking trash that the world had thrown away, and finding something valuable and useful for his glory.

I had many opportunities during the week to engage the students
in activities, and to listen to and talk to them. I began to realize what it
must be like for Jesus to listen to my dreams, feelings, and concerns.
I was encouraged to see students working together as teams, helping
each other.

But I was learning more about myself, too. I felt the Holy Spirit giving me strength to love more and judge less. Maybe it was me who God
was changing and taking me out to deeper water so I could get to know
Him more. God is truly amazing. As I drove the bus from the retreat,
I heard God ask me a question: "Do you think you have done a good
job being patient with all of these students, staff, and adults this time
around?" I answered, "Yes. I didn't lose my temper, nor was I quick
to be judgmental toward anyone." I felt deserving of a solid pat on my
back because of what I had accomplished during the retreat.

But God wasn't done talking to me. In my spirit, He said, "Yes, you
have done a good job in my will, but I want you to multiply your patience a million times, so you can understand my love for humanity.
Immediately, I felt a sense of smallness all around me because I was in
His presence. It was then that the Holy Spirit moved my heart to hear
His request. "I desire for you to write a song for me and it should be
called 'Falling Away From Me.' I am God, and my mercy and patience
is forever with those who do not yet know me. I will wait on the bigot,
homosexual, adulterer, the rich, the poor, beggar, thief, and the liar.

I'm never moved by the sin of people, for my love changes everything."

Suddenly, my lips began to hum the sound of the horn that would be played in the beginning of the song. As I drove along, I listened to His voice directing me to each line of the song. I found myself singing along to what God was giving to me through the Holy Spirit. It must have looked strange to the students who saw me humming and singing, with no music to accompany this madness. But I just kept listening and singing each line out, with no doubt in my mind that God was doing something remarkable.

When we arrived back at the school campus, I was relieved to notice how much energy I had left. Also, the song that God had shared with me was finished with every beat, sound, and instrument which was to be used to glorify His name. It was all in my head, and I could not wait to get home to put it down on paper.

19

FALLING AWAY FROM ME

WHEN WE GOT HOME FROM THE RETREAT, MY WIFE WANTED US TO GET UNPACKED, DO LAUNDRY AND PUT THINGS IN ORDER. I found myself pleading with her about this new song that I had to complete for God. Believe it or not, she allowed me to go upstairs and have my time alone to work on the song. I guess over 19 years of marriage, she has gotten used to me telling her about doing things for God, and she knows by now God is up to something.

With pencil in hand and God as the author, I began writing out the song that would change me and the others that would hear the words of the song. It all fit together like no other song I've ever written.

At this point, I wondered why God would choose me to write this song when there are so many great Christian artists out there. God gave me a clear answer on this matter: "The reason I chose you is because anybody that would meet you would know that it came directly from Me."

With the song done, I thought that God would give me a break, so I could turn my full attention to start coaching the varsity boys' and middle school basketball teams. But He made it clear that this would take priority over the basketball season due to the fact that His timing is perfect and He alone would be my strength. So, I prayed for guidance concerning who would sing the song, what instruments were to be used, and who would fund such a project like this, that He had already predestined to be a blessing. Not to mention patience and endurance to make it through such a project while coaching two teams.

God made it clear to me who would sing the song, so I called my good friend Jerry Kemper, whom I had known since my days doing the bible study at Charlotte Latin School. He was the music teacher at Central Academy at Lake Park. He had a local studio not too far from the school where he gave private music lessons. Jerry said earlier that he would love to collaborate on a song or two.

The first meeting in his studio was awesome, because Jerry allowed me to share the vision that God had given me at the retreat. He was an excellent listener and a great musician. We spent three to four hours in his studio getting the melody and chorus together. Before leaving the studio, we prayed together, and I knew God was moving to bring about His will in this matter.

Jerry and I met several more times to perfect the music. Now, we were ready to record the song, with Jerry singing and playing guitar. Two other musicians, Randy Johnson and Jason York, collaborated with us. What an incredible moment for me to hear this song that God had birthed from heaven.

Jason made some copies of the recording, so that I could be ready for the next step that God would have me to take. On the way home. Jerry and I listened to the song again. It was even more amazing to hear this time around, because God began to speak again to me about the next step. I asked Jerry what he thought about bringing in more musicians and making a better recording that would be radio ready. Jerry said musicians are not free and it would cost a lot of money. However, if I could get an electric guitar player, French horn player, bass player, drummer, keyboard player, and acoustic guitar player, the song could be brought to the next level. Studio time would be costly, but if the musicians rehearsed the song outside of the studio before the recording, it would definitely cost less.

I felt more overwhelmed. God reminded me of His plan, but it's always a leap of faith from one moment to the next. Thankfully, I had resources to find musicians, but God told me to tell each one that He had need of them and for them to work free of charge. After church on a Sunday, I approached each one of the musicians told them exactly what God said to tell them, and believe it or not, it worked!

Later, I told Jerry that I got together the band members that he re-quested, and that they would all work free of charge. He was astounded. He said no musicians work for free! But I told him again that God put these musicians in place for a time such as this. I gave him the list with their contact information, so he could schedule the first rehearsal time.

At that first rehearsal, I was watching everything Jerry and the band were doing. Without realizing it, I began crying when they started playing, because it struck me that this song was a reflection of my whole life.

The last rehearsals came at the end of the year, and we needed to be in the studio recording in early January. But in order to do this, I needed two things: someone to pay for the studio time, and someone to pay for the production of the CDs.

Jason York gave me a contact at a studio, and according to him Jake was an expert. Without hesitation, I called him and introduced myself and explained to him what Jerry and I had discussed about studio time. Jake said that he did have an opening in early January, and for each hour in the studio it would be a fee of $100. This was a little alarming, because I did not have a dime to spend. Then we talked about the price of the CDs, and who would be designing the cover. I learned that doing one song was not to my advantage because most people do a full CD of songs for the cost I was looking to produce just one song. To make 500 CDs, it would cost $850, and another couple hundred if Jake's company were to design the CD cover. This was more than I could take in, because I had not thought that far ahead. At this point, I needed another miracle, because what I heard was a little disheartening to say the least.

During this time, I went to God in prayer and He directed me to take the demo CD to a close friend of mine, whose son I had coached in basketball many years ago. He was a successful businessman. I told him the story of the song that God inspired me to write. I asked if he might be willing to give toward making either the recording time possible or CDs happen – or just tell me to get lost. He set up a time for me to come by to meet with him.

When I got to Mr. Stump's office, he said he was ready to listen. He had talked with his wife, and they remembered a song I wrote in eulogy to a student who had passed away, and it was played at her funeral. They also remembered a graduation song that I had written for Charlotte Latin. After listening to "Falling Away From Me," Mr. Stump asked how much I needed to record in the studio. When I told him, he opened his wallet and gave me the entire amount on the spot. I said thank you as tears filled my eyes. I went home praising God because I was more encouraged now than ever before.

20

GOD'S CRISIS
MANAGEMENT PLAN

AFTER TALKING WITH JERRY, I REALIZED I MIGHT HAVE A CRISIS ON MY HANDS. The last rehearsal was coming up in three days, on a Friday when I had to coach two basketball games back to back, and take care of some logistics concerning the rehearsal. God did not give me a clear answer concerning that Friday, but instead gave me another donor to call. Mr. Mathisen was the founder of Lake Park Academy and the developer of the Lake Park community itself. I considered him a mentor, because he inspired me to dream big when I was hired as athletic director for the new Central Academy At Lake Park. I had met him about 12 years ago when my wife had started working for his school. He had helped me with a big project at my home, and I remember many times going to lunch with him, so I could just receive more wisdom from this Christian man.

Before calling him about the song, I had consulted with my wife so she could be in prayer, because I realized that his wife would play a pivotal role in their decision to support my project. When I did call, he agreed to listen, but said he and his wife wouldn't do anything without praying about it first.

At his home, Mr. Mathisen and his wife listened first to recordings of the other songs I had written, before I played "Falling Away From Me" for them. Afterward, he told me that he was a music director at a church before becoming a land developer. He appreciated the different styles of music that I shared with him. Then Mr. Mathisen said that they could see many people being saved from this song because of the message. When I told him how much money I needed, they agreed to pray and get back to me in the next day or so.

I arrived back at my office after lunch the next day to hear a message from Mr. Mathisen on my voice mail. They would be bringing a check to my office that afternoon. All I could do was praise the Lord, because all the money was in place to fulfill God's purpose for this song. I hope the students and teachers didn't hear the noise that I was making in my office, but I didn't really care, because it was another miracle moment for me.

Not long after, I met with a professional photographer that provided pictures for the CD cover. And through a godly couple that I knew, I met a graphic designer – a Christian – who meticulously produced the cover for the CD. God was working in every step to get the CD out to those who need to hear the message of the song.

The day had finally arrived for us to go into the studio to record the song "Falling Away From Me." I was overwhelmed with this dream that God was bringing to fruition. I cried several times on my drive to the recording studio in Rock Hill. Ironically, as I drove my car into South Carolina, I passed the area where Boys Town used to be located. I could not help but remember those ten years of my childhood spent there.

I arrived about 7:45 a.m. so I could enjoy every moment of what God was about to do right before my eyes as we recorded. I sat down with Jake to discuss the contract agreement which would allow us to use the studio from 8:30 a.m. until 6:00 p.m. I was well-prepared for any business transaction because of all the planning that I had put in with my wife and with Jerry Kemper. I could take a deep breath because all the numbers fit.

God gave me a miracle to watch that day, happening right before my eyes. Every verse being sung and instrument being played was a reminder that God had taken this abandoned child who was raised in a boys' home for ten years to write a song that would save souls around the world just because of His grace and mercy. But the question that kept coming to me throughout the day as the project unfolded was: "How is God going to get this out to them?"

At the end of the day, everyone was extremely tired. I was thankful to the band members, Jerry and Jake, for being a part of this miracle.

As we left the studio, I asked them to stay in prayer because God would reveal to me what the next step would be for His song, "Falling Away From Me."

For the next couple of days, I found myself being anxious waiting for Jake's call to tell me he had mixed the song, and it was ready for Jerry and me to go back out to the studio and listen to it. I threw myself into working even more with my basketball teams. It was a remarkable season by any standard, since the varsity record to that point was 14-0, and the middle school team was undefeated 10-0. I stayed busy working extra in practice with both teams while checking daily on my players' grades and holding team meetings at lunch. Consequently, I found this time challenging being a coach, father, and husband.

I finally heard from Jake that the mix was done, and Jerry and I made plans to go to the studio that weekend. It was hard, because there were a lot of things to be done before this week was over, but with God's help, I was able to focus on the moment. I had two games on Tuesday and two games on Friday. As I got my tired body into bed on Friday night, the only thing on my mind was listening to the remix in the studio the following day. Still, I fell to my knees to thank God for bringing me through the week, as God reminded me the best was yet to come.

We listened to the new recording, which sounded amazing, but Jerry thought that a couple of things needed to be tweaked and Jake agreed. Jake said that it would be done in a matter of hours, and we could come back later that day to listen. Jerry and I did not mind at all, because we both wanted this project finished.

We were extremely pleased with the changes. Jake said the master and other copies would be ready within two weeks, and "Falling Away From Me" would be done. On the way back from the studio, Jerry said God was not done using this song for His glory — that this was only the beginning, and I agreed.

21

INTRODUCING "FALLING AWAY FROM ME"

I FELT LIKE EVERYTHING WAS FALLING INTO PLACE. Five hundred CDs would be ready at some point, and the basketball teams were finishing strong. I was still waiting on God to give me the answer to how He would get the word out for His song. Then it happened.

During the most hectic day of the week, I received a call in the gym office. "Hello, this is Langston Wertz. I would like to do a phone interview with you, so I can do a story on your team, and about your life. Do you have time to talk?" Langston was a sports writer for The Charlotte Observer newspaper. How would God get the story out about His song? It happened that day, with students yelling in the background, in a ten-minute interview which was totally unexpected.

I told him about our overall record for the season and gave names of our impact players. We talked about my position at our school and my wife's. At the end of the interview, I told him about the song that God had inspired me to write, and that I would like for it to be a part of the story, if possible. He said that he would mention it, and to make sure that the photographer gets a picture of the CD when she comes out to take the picture for the article. As I got off the phone, I felt the presence of the Holy Spirit in the room, as tears of joy streamed down my face. Then I realized even more this was truly God's song, because He was still working miracles right before my eyes that were humanly impossible.

On Monday, I called The Charlotte Observer and spoke with the photographer that Langston had referred to me. We made an appointment for the following Saturday – and the CDs were scheduled to be ready by then.

When the CDs were ready, I went to the studio to get them, and cried because it was all coming together in God's timing. I told Jake that God had great plans for His song.

Deidre came from the Observer to take the photos for the article. After the photo shoot, she said she would send me over the pictures by email so that I could keep them for future use.

After the photo shoot, I just made my mind up to focus on the present and not think about how God was working behind the scenes. So, with both basketball teams nearing the end of their seasons, I gave all of my energy and focus to my athletes. Both teams won both conference championships and their tournament championships. It was a remarkable season, even with all of the extra activities that God had called me to be involved in. I surely felt my cup was running over as I reflected back over the season. There were many times I did not soar but run, and there were other times that I could only walk. However, through it all, God was faithful in keeping me and delivering me in every situation.

The article came out in the Observer the following Sunday. On Saturday night, I was excited, but too tired to fight sleep any longer. Before we went to sleep, Mildred and I agreed we were blessed, and would not let anything ever change who we are in Christ. We just wanted to continue to love everybody and walk humbly before God.

In the morning after we had quiet prayer times, I went out the door to retrieve the newspaper while Mildred started breakfast. "Praise the Lord!," I said as I gazed at the article with a picture of my family with the CD in our hands. Mildred said, "God is good, because how could this happen to us when there are so many other people who are more newsworthy?" I knew that it happened because of God's song and His desire to have mercy and to send out His message of love one more time.

Central Academy at Lake Park High School athletic director and basketball coach Dale Similton poses with his wife, Mildred, and children Joseph, left, and Daniel in the school's gym. He's come a long way since growing up an orphan in Charlotte.

Lake Park coach reaches goals: Good job, good family, good life

LANGSTON WERTZ JR.

Lake Park High coach Dale Similton considers himself, as he puts it, "extra lucky." He says he has most everything he always wanted:

A good job, a good family, a good life.

Similton, a devout Christian, won his fourth consecutive Charlotte Area Christian Athletic Association conference championship last week with a 79-51 win over Carolina Christian.

His team finished the season 21-1.

He said he can't imagine being anywhere else. And it's good to see a good man land in a good place. As a kid, Similton was abandoned by his parents along with his six brother and sisters. They were split among foster homes.

Similton and two of his brothers were adopted by a Kannapolis woman named Lola Neal, and they lived with her for five years. Neal was getting up in age and couldn't care for the boys anymore

The boys ended up at a youth home called Boys Town, outside Pineville. Similton stayed there for 10 years, through his time at Pineville Elementary and Quail Hollow Junior High.

In high school at South Mecklenburg, Similton played for legendary basketball coach Dave Price and was a star wide receiver who eventually became an All-American at Mars Hill, determined to not let his tough circumstances hinder his ability to reach his goals: good job, good family, good life.

After college, Similton eventually got into coaching and once led Charlotte Latin's middle school team to a 17-1 record and studied under one of the state's best-ever coaches, Jerry Faulkner, who won more than 700 games.

After Latin, Similton helped upstart Covenant Day make the playoffs two years in a row and eventually got the job at Lake Park, where his wife is an assistant principal and his two kids attend school.

The family lives in the neighborhood in Indian Trail where the school is located. And this is where Similton thinks he was called to be.

"I think God wanted me to build an athletic program," said Similton, who has recorded a song about his faith, "Falling Away From Me," that is being released at his church, Central Church of God, and several others. "I attend-

Coach Similton recorded a song, "Falling Away From Me," which will be released at Central Church of God, where he has been a member for 16 years, and other churches.

ed Central Church for 16 years, and when they bought out Lake Park, an athletic job was open. When I met with them, I knew I'd make a good fit."

Similton's first team won a championship and he's won a championship every year since. Similton also coaches Lake Park's middle school team, which finished 17-1.

"It's amazing what's happened to me," Similton said. "I've come a long way. I am very blessed. I'm very fortunate to do what I do every day. I love these kids and they've

grown so tremendously. We have kids who may be missing a father or a mother that I deal with every day. The kids just need a touch of love.

"God shaped me as a child, God shaped me at (Charlotte) Latin and Covenant Day to do what I'm doing now. I can't imagine doing anything else."

And why would he?

He has a good job, a good family. A good life.

Wertz: 704-512-9716; lwertz@charlotteobserver.com

Lake Park High coach Dale Similton considers himself, as he puts it, "extra lucky." He says he has most everything he always wanted:

A good job, a good family, a good life.

Similton, a devout Christian, won his fourth consecutive Charlotte Area Christian Athletic Association conference championship last week with a 79-51 win over Carolina Christian.

His team finished the season 21-1.

He said he can't imagine being anywhere else. And it's good to see a good man land in a good place. As a kid, Similton was abandoned by his parents along with his six brothers and sisters. They were split among foster homes.

Similton and two of his brothers were adopted by a Kannapolis woman named Lola Neal, and they lived with her for five years. Neal was getting up in age and couldn't care for the boys anymore.

The boys ended up at a youth home called Boys Town, outside Pineville. Similton stayed there for 10 years, through his time at Pineville Elementary and Quail Hollow Junior High.

In high school at South Mecklenburg, Similton played for legendary basketball coach Dave Price and was a star wide receiver who eventually became an Honorable Mentioned All-American at Mars Hill, determined to not let his tough circumstances hinder his ability to reach his goals: good job, good family, good life.

After college, Similton eventually got into coaching and once led

Charlotte Latin's middle school team to a 17-1 record and studied under one of the state's best-ever coaches, Jerry Faulkner, who won more than 700 games.

After Latin, Similton helped upstart Covenant Day make the playoffs two years in a row and eventually got the job at Lake Park, where his wife is an assistant principal and his two kids attend school.

The family lives in the neighborhood in Indian Trail where the school is located. And this is where Similton thinks he was called to be.

"I think God wanted me to build an athletic program," said Similton, who has recorded a song about his faith, "Falling Away From Me." "I attended Central Church for 16 years, and when they bought out Lake Park, the athletic job was open. When I met with them, I knew I'd make a good fit."

Similton's first team won a championship and he's won the championship three straight years since. Similton also coaches Lake Park's middle school team, which finished 17-1.

"It's amazing what's happened to me," Similton said. "I've come a long way. I am blessed. I'm fortunate to do what I do every day. I love these kids and they've grown so tremendously. We have kids who may be missing a father or a mother that I deal with every day. The kids just need a touch of love.

"God shaped me as a child, God shaped me at (Charlotte) Latin and Covenant Day to do what I'm doing now. I can't imagine doing

anything else."

And why would he?

He has a good job, a good family.

A good life.

("Lake Park coach reaches goals: Good job, good family, good life"
by Langston Wertz, Jr. Reprinted with permission from The Char-
lotte Observer.)

FALLING AWAY FROM ME

So, here I am looking over the ocean as the sun shines

down on me, while time reminds me of my fears.

Jesus can you save me, will you wait for me? I

find myself falling, falling away from me.

So, here I am, in my moment of truth hoping

for a miracle without a prayer.

Always thinking about my past never realizing whose I am.

Jesus can you save me, will you wait for me? I

find myself falling, falling away from me.

So, here I am living in my Kingdom, still

missing the perfect love that could save me.

Jesus can you save me, will you wait for me? I

find myself falling, falling away from me.

Jesus can you save me? There are no dreams to lie to me.

Jesus can you save me? Time is passing and grace has left me.

Jesus can you save me? The world is spinning all around me.

Jesus can you save me? Sin is my only

friend and it won't let me win.

Jesus can you save me? Fighting the shadows.

So, here I am falling, falling away from me.

Jesus can you save me, will you wait for me?

Now, I'm falling at your feet.

22

GOD'S REVELATION IS MY SALVATION

A COUPLE OF YEARS HAVE PASSED SINCE THIS ARTICLE WAS PUBLISHED, AND GOD IS STILL DOING A "NEW THING" IN MY FAMILY. I realize more and more that God's revelation is my salvation. As it states in Acts 1:5, "He appeared to his disciples after His death and made it clear to them to go to Jerusalem and wait in the Upper Room until the Holy Spirit came down upon them to give them power." Sometimes I find myself waiting to hear God's voice, and He does not speak until a period of waiting has passed. At the end of the 2013-2014 school year, my wife prayerfully decided to step down as Upper School Principal and do College and Career Counseling in 2014-15, which would be part-time.

Consequently, I found myself feeling as it states in 2 Corinthians 4:8, "We are perplexed but not in despair, we are pressed down but never crushed, we are persecuted but never abandoned." I really could not comprehend in the flesh why my wife was not happy being Principal, but rather desired to be a college and career counselor. She has been blessed to do a superb job in both areas, and she did make it clear to me on several occasions that she wanted to spend more time with Joseph as he goes into his junior year and be available to take him on college visits.

During this time, Daniel was excelling on the middle school basketball team, which finished with 20 wins and no losses. I really enjoyed coaching him through his three years in the Middle School, and I looked forward to coaching him on the varsity level. Joseph had a spectacular season on the varsity boys team. He was one of the top assist leaders in Union County, and among the top ten scorers. While the overall athletic program at Central Academy flourished throughout the 2014-15 school year, one of the major highlights was when ESPN Basketball Sports Analyst Jay Bilas came and spoke to our students, school, and community. I really believed that God was moving my family, school, and community to new spiritual levels.

My wife, as she later shared with me, was busy praying and seeking God's will on whether to remain at Central Academy. I was in a state of shock, because I had just gotten used to her not being Upper School Principal, and now she stated that God was moving her in a different direction altogether. Immediately, I found myself wanting God to reveal His revelation to me so I could understand what He was doing. It made very little sense to me. Why God would choose to uproot my wife when all I've ever prayed for was to work professionally with her was beyond my understanding. At this point, she informed me that Daniel would need to be moved to another school the next year so his academic needs could be better met. I felt like Satan was attacking my family and that my wife was very confused on God's true Revelation in this matter.

I started fasting from breakfast until lunch for several weeks seeking God's ordained will in this matter. As a result of me humbling myself before the Lord over a period of time, He began to reveal His power and made clear to me His revelation in this matter. In April, my wife had a wreck in our Ford van, which was reported to me as I was teaching my PE class. Also, it was communicated that I needed get there as soon as I could, because she had hit her head in the accident. My thoughts got the best of me, because I could only imagine the worst, and even though I prayed, my heart wavered.

The accident happened about three miles away from the school, but it seemed like an eternity for me to get there. I could not stop the tears from coming down my face as I made my way to the scene of the accident. However, I felt the presence of the Holy Spirit comforting me because this was the first time that I had been in a situation like this concerning my wife. After arriving there, the medics and police officers seemed to have everything under control (except my emotions). It was during this time that God said to me, "Do you trust me with your wife?

Then let go." As I checked on her, I noticed she was still strapped into her seat belt, and she was complaining to the medics that her neck and the back of her head were in pain. They did an excellent job of attending to her needs as they placed her in the ambulance and took her to the nearest hospital.

God reminded me that I was not in control of anything, but it was by faith and prayer that His mercy and grace is renewed every morning. As it states in Psalm 30:5 "His anger lasts but a moment. In His favor is life. Tears endure during the night, but joy cometh in the morning." My wife was able to leave the hospital that night with only a prescription to be filled for the pain she was experiencing. Also, she had to endure therapy for her neck for several weeks. I'm sad to say it did not go as well for our van. It was considered to be totaled, but the accident was deemed not my wife's fault, and we were able to buy another vehicle later.

This was a very difficult time for me, but I needed to go through this to understand God's will for my wife and Daniel. He definitely showed me in more ways than one that He desired for my wife and Daniel to go to another school. My wife was offered a job as a high school Guidance Counselor at Covenant Day at this time. Also, Daniel tested and got accepted at the same school, and the financial package was perfect for our budget. As I reflected on my own time spent working at Covenant Day seven years prior, I was reminded of what God stated in Proverbs 22:1 "A good name is more desirable than great riches, and to be esteemed is better than silver or gold." Now, my wife and Daniel are welcome there, because through Christ's power, I loved much while I was there. That's why when I close my eyes tonight, I can rest in peace in knowing that Joseph and I will be together at Central Academy, while Mom and Daniel will be attending Covenant Day School in the 2015-16 school year. This brings me back to my point that God's revelation is my salvation. As Paul stated in Philippians 4:19, "My God will meet all of my needs according to the riches of His glory in Christ Jesus."

23

GOD'S THOUGHTS ARE FAR GREATER

COUPLE OF WEEKS LATER, MY WIFE SHOWED ME ANOTHER REVELATION CONCERNING JOSEPH BEING A PART OF THE COVENANT EXODUS, TOO. I was at a loss for words and very frustrated with the game that God was playing. During this time, the only thought that made sense to me was keeping Joseph safe with me, so I did not have to look bad in front of Central Academy families, students, and community. To say the least, I was absorbed with my reputation and how this would look to my superior and others. Suddenly, I began to distance myself from my own family, because I felt betrayed, and none of them seemed to care. Many times, I tried to persuade Joseph to stay. Also, I let him know that he would get very little newspaper coverage because of

Covenant Day's tough basketball schedule. He would have to start over again rebuilding his reputation.

Even though this was all true, I knew deep in my heart that God was testing me again to see if I would let go and let Him take control. I agonized over this decision so much until I felt all of my fasting was done in vain. Still, I kept on fasting, trying to be faithful to my God, because He states in 2 Timothy 2:13, "If we are faithless, He will always be faithful because He will not deny Himself." I found myself in a confused state not knowing what God wanted, but knowing what I needed to happen. This is when God sent me on a mission to drive back to Boys Town, so He could remind me of His goodness and mercy. Upon my arrival at the boys home, I did not see any signs that led me to believe that the boys home ever existed. However, what I did see was a school at the entrance of the property, and when I finally arrived at the old Boys Town gym, I noticed a sign that read Park 51 Recreation Center.

At this point, I felt home again with tons of memories flooding my mind, but most importantly, God was there filling me with His Holy Spirit. It was then I realized that my journey was not over at Central Academy, but I needed to endure the race set before me. As it states in Ecclesiastes 9:11, "The race does not go to the fastest nor the battle to the strong, nor does food always go to the wise, or riches go to those in power or favor to the skilled; but it's in God's timing that all things happen." As, I drove back home to see my family, I had a different mindset, which was to commit my decision concerning Joseph to the

Lord and to be obedient to His will.

As I face this new year knowing Daniel, Joseph, as well as Mildred will no longer be with me at Central Academy, I put my faith in God knowing that He stated in Romans 11:36 "Yes, in all things we are more than conquerors through him who loved and died for us." So, there can be no turning back for me because I truly believe that God has greater work yet to be done at Central Academy. Therefore, I will be strong and of good courage, knowing that the battle is not mine but is the Lord's. My prayer each day will be that God would bless each student, faculty, staff, and administrator's day. Still, He has charged me to minister to His other sons and daughters, as He did with His disciple and His mother at the foot of the cross. I am reminded that He stated in Deuteronomy 31:6 "Be strong of a good courage. Do not be afraid of what people will do or say, for the Lord goes before you; He will never leave you or forsake you." Now, I too must be about my Father's business.

24

GOD'S EXALTATION IS TIMELESS

IN THE MONTH OF SEPTEMBER DURING MY 52ND BIRTHDAY, MY SISTER DONNA CALLED ME AND STATED THAT SHE HAD A SURPRISE FOR ME WHICH I WOULD LOVE. At that moment, I did not think too much about it with all of the other things going on in my family life. Eventually, I went to visit her with Daniel and Joseph to share in this good news and to check on her declining health. As usual, my boys and I gave her hugs and told her how much we loved her. I could tell that she was filled with the Holy Spirit, as she began to share thoughts from her heart. She began by telling me how proud she was concerning my life's achievements and family life. I was overwhelmed by my sister's kindness and her sincere words which touched my very soul. At this time, the demeanor of my boys was one of grace and respect, as they observed the moment.

Afterward, I told her how proud I was of her since high school for being courageous in her battle against breast cancer and for trusting God for allowing her to give birth to two boys that were now young men. The doctors made clear more than once that she could not give birth because of her overall health condition. I was always in awe of how God allowed this to come to pass and the miracle of it all.

Suddenly, she stated that she had waited a long time to give me this gift as if she knew the hour was at hand. So, without hesitation she brought out this big package that was concealed in nice wrapping paper. I had no idea what was inside. Even if I could have guessed a million times, I would never have even come close. She gave it to me along with the command for me to open the package which I did with great anticipation. As I opened the package, I had no doubt that my sister loved me and maybe she knew something that I did not know. Underneath the wrapping paper was my old football game jersey from Mars Hill College that I had given to her after a football game about thirty years ago. I remembered it was a beautiful sunny day, and we had just won a big game. She had driven up from Concord, North Carolina along with one of her girlfriends. I thought it would be special to give her my old jersey because of our bond.

Now, thirty years later she was giving it back to me mounted in a beautiful picture frame. I was speechless to say the least, knowing that love never stops giving. As tears filled my eyes, I could not help but reflect on those years that I spent training to be a warrior for the Lord.

The words that were spoken to Esther echoed loudly to me, "For a time such as this" Esther 4:14. I was so thankful that my sister kept her promise for always being there for me.

This event was definitely a spiritual one, because in early October God told me to call Mars Hill University to inquire about my jersey being retired. Although I never played pro football, this idea was a long shot. After talking with the Athletic Director, he stated that players' jerseys are never retired; however, outstanding football players are sometimes voted into the Mars Hill Hall of Fame. He told me that voting is done by committee, and once a player's name is submitted, it can never be taken out of the process. Sooner or later, you will have the opportunity to be voted into the Hall of Fame. At that point, I asked if I would be considered for such an honor, and he stated that the time for voting was coming up in the next couple of weeks and my name would be considered. As it states in Matthew 7:7, "Ask, and it shall be given you; seek, and ye shall find; knock, and it shall be opened unto you."

In late October, I received a voice mail message from Mars Hill University concerning this matter. A longtime friend of mine who had played football with me who was now a coach up at Mars Hill called and left a message. He said he had some good news for me concerning getting into the Hall of Fame and that I should give him a call back. After listening to this message, I started praising God with tears of joy in my eyes. I cared less about what the people around me were thinking, because at that point my cup was overflowing.

When I called my friend, he said "Congratulations on being voted into the Mars Hill Football Hall Of Fame." I was overwhelmed to hear those words, because I thought too much time had passed and no one remembered. However, in that moment God reminded me that thirty years is like a second to Him. Also, God made it clear that through it all, He was testing and humbling me. For He said in Matthew 23:12, "For those who seek to be exalted He will humble, and those who seek to be humble He will exalt them." I shared this good news with my wife and family. Daniel and Joseph were full of joy, while Mildred gave me a kiss and hug and said she was proud of me.

Mars Hill athletic public relations department requested that I fill out a biographical information sheet concerning my years at Mars Hill, along with an update on my family and career. Also, they asked that I send any team or individual records so they could compare with what was in their possession. It was easy to fill out the biographical information with the form they sent. However, remembering old records after thirty years was a major problem. But God had already solved that problem several weeks earlier when I met with my good friend and mentor, Doug Youngblood, at his office. He had given me the box that was filled with my old Mars Hill write-ups and other information that I had left at his house close to thirty years ago. To this day, I'm puzzled by why he did not throw that box away, instead of keeping it.

Now, I could answer all of the questions that the Athletic Department had requested of me without any doubt. Over the next few weeks, through emails, mail, and phone contacts everything seemed to fall into place concerning being inducted into the Mars Hill University

Hall Of Fame. The Athletic Department notified me that on Saturday, November 7th, during halftime of the Mars Hill Football Game that the 1985 Championship Football team would be recognized. I was delighted, because that was my team, and I loved those men who shared in that time of my life. On that same day, Mars Hill would allow me to invite several family members to a luncheon before the game, so all of the Championship Team members and Inductees could enjoy a time together. At halftime of the Mars Hill football game, the Hall of Fame inductees would be recognized in front of the Mars Hill home crowd. Each inductee would be given a plaque with their overall accomplishments on them, presented by the President of the University.

Later, a reporter from The Charlotte Observer called concerning the Mars Hill Athletic Department press release which had been sent, so that the community at large would be able to share in this moment. On this day, I was reminded of Isaiah 61:7: "Instead of shame God will give you a double portion, instead of disgrace He will give you an inheritance."

25

A Day of Honor
Reserved By Christ

ON SUNDAY NOVEMBER 1, 2015, MY FAMILY AND I WENT TO CHURCH AS USUAL, AND AFTERWARD SPENT TIME GROCERY SHOPPING AT WALMART. After arriving home, we prayed together and started unloading groceries while Mildred began breakfast. I finished my duties and headed upstairs to start looking over my assignment for next week. I noticed that I had a phone message left by a number that I did not recognize. Upon listening to the call, I derived that it was a sportswriter from the Charlotte Observer who was calling to do a story on the upcoming Hall of Fame event up at Mars Hill University. He requested that I call him back for a 30 to 35-minute interview concerning me being inductee into the Hall of Fame. I went into my prayer closet to talk things over with God, because I wanted the Holy Spirit to speak through me and not words of the flesh.

I finished praying and gave the sports writer a call back to listen and share my thoughts on the subject matter at hand. I was amazed at his questions about the beginning of my journey and his ability to draw out emotions that I did not know that I had been feeling or thinking about this upcoming event. I told him that Christ was the number one factor in my overall success. Also, I had established a foundation on the three C's which are Courage, Confidence, and Character that was evident in my two brothers, Ron and Wesley, growing up with them at Boys Town in Pineville, North Carolina. The question that caused me to reflect most deeply was the one about my sister Donna. He asked me about who inspired me on my journey the most? I told him about my baby sister who had always been my number one fan from junior high, high school and throughout my college career.

Perhaps this was the reason I gave her one of my old college football jersey No. 22 after a football game up at Mars Hill. It was the same number that I had worn throughout my high school career. I thought that she would enjoy it and probably keep it for a short time period. However, on my fifty-second birthday in September she gave it back to me mounted in a beautiful picture frame accompanied with a ceremony in front of my two boys up at her house. I never thought that she would hold on to that jersey or give it back to me, especially with this miracle event forthcoming which neither of us could have forseen.

I finished my phone interview with the writer still thinking about why I was driven by the three C's that I had shared with him — Courage, Confidence and Character. Also, what inspired me to continue to try to be a good person and serve others? On Monday, November 2, around 5:00 a.m., I woke up crying and groaning in my spirit, as the Holy Spirit revealed unto me the true purpose of my faith walk. After reflecting on the emotional questions that The Charlotte Observer writer had asked me, God revealed that He used my sister Donna, who had been diagnosed with breast cancer in high school. Today, Donna struggles to walk and is in a tremendous amount of pain due to the spread of the cancer. I realize that my true purpose is to love, serve, and to inspire others to trust God. And most importantly, God wanted me to write a song and a book entitled "Falling Away From Me." It was always about my sister Donna, my number one fan and friend.

On November 4th, 2015, the following article ran online in The Charlotte Observer. I'm still amazed at the power of the Living God.

❖ ❖ ❖

LAKE PARK

Mars Hill hall of fame calls Similton's name

BY JAY EDWARDS
Correspondent

Dale Similton was 5 years old when his parents abandoned him and his six siblings.

Similton spent 1972-1982 at Boys' Town in Pineville (now Elon Homes and Schools for Children in Charlotte), where his older brothers, Larry and Wendell also stayed. Similton excelled in what he describes as a "a supportive, Christian environment."

He became a standout student-athlete at South Mecklenburg High, where he played basketball, track and football. As a wide receiver, he earned a spot on the Mars Hill College (now University) football team. Similton set records

for most receiving yards in a season (940), touchdowns in a game (three) and receiving touchdowns in a season (12).

Similton again is in the school's spotlight as he is among the 2015 class going into the Mars Hill Sports Hall of Fame. The ceremony is set for Nov. 7.

Similton said the experience is special because he gets to share it with his family, including his wife of 20 years, Dr. Mildred

SEE SIMILTON, 2U

COURTESY OF ANNEZELLE JOUBERT

Dale Similton holds the No. 22 jersey he wore during his record-setting days at Mars Hill College. As a senior he gave the jersey to his sister, Donna. Thirty years later she gave it back to him, on his birthday last Sept. 18.

Dale Similton was 5 years old when his parents abandoned him and his six siblings.

Similton spent 1972-1982 at Boys' Town in Pineville (now Elon Homes and Schools for Children in Charlotte), where his older brothers, Larry and Wendell also stayed. Similton excelled in what he describes as "a supportive, Christian environment."

He became a standout student-athlete at South Mecklenburg High, where he played basketball, track and football. As a wide receiver, he earned a spot on the Mars Hill College (now University) football team. Similton set records for most receiving yards in a season (940), touchdowns in a game (three) and receiving touchdowns in a season (12).

Similton again is in the school's spotlight as he is among the 2015 class going into the Mars Hill Sports Hall of Fame. The ceremony is set for Nov. 7.

Similton said the experience is special because he gets to share it with his family, including his wife of 20 years, Dr. Mildred Similton, his sons, Joseph and Daniel, and his younger sister, Donna Rucker.

"It is very humbling to be inducted into the Hall of Fame," Similton said. "When I first got the call that I'd be going into the Hall of Fame, it was overwhelming.

"For me being an abandoned child growing up, and now to get to share something like this with my wife and children and my sister, Donna, who was always my No. 1 fan, is hard to put into words."

Giving Back

Now 52, Similton has spent the past 30 years helping others as an athletic director, coach and mentor.

After graduating from Mars Hill in 1985, Similton returned to Elon Home for Children in Charlotte to serve as a house parent.

"It was very rewarding to be able to go back to the place where I grew and help others facing the same kind of struggles like I did," Similton said. "God has blessed me with a passion for helping children. The misery I suffered growing up as an abandoned child, ended up turning into a ministry for me to help kids who grew up just like myself."

After five years at Elon Home for Children, Similton decided he also could help young people as a teacher and coach. He landed at Charlotte Latin School in 1991.

Similton worked 15 years as a history teacher, junior varsity football coach and varsity basketball assistant, under legendary Charlotte Latin coach Jerry Faulkner.

He also helped start and run Latin's intramural program, where he often created games for the kids, while inviting guest speakers like Carolina Panthers' standouts John Kasay and Steve Smith.

"Dale (Similton) has an incredible passion and zest for life and for helping kids, and he had a boundless energy to do so," said Debbie Lamb, who, for 21 years, has been the head of Charlotte Latin middle school. "Because he came from a tough situation as a child, he appreciates family from his wife and children to his colleagues to his students."

Similton also has served as the Covenant Day boys' basketball coach (2006-08). And now he is athletic director and head boys' basketball coach for high school varsity and middle school programs at Central Academy at Lake Park. Similton helped build the basketball programs, and now they are annual contenders in the Charlotte Area Christian Athletic Association. He also runs "Similton Faith, Hope and Love" summer camps each June and July.

Sister as Inspiration

Donna Similton Rucker would go anywhere to watch Dale play basketball or football. She also survived breast cancer as a high school student at A.L. Brown High School in Kannapolis.

"My younger sister was a major source of motivation for me, because I saw all that she was going through and I wanted to do something for her," Similton said.

As a senior, he gave Donna his No. 22 Mars Hill football jersey. Dale and Donna shared a special moment this year on Sept. 18 — Dale's birthday. Donna gave back the jersey to Dale. He now has it framed in his house.

"I couldn't believe she still had that jersey after all these years," Similton said. "She always believed in me and still means a lot to me today."

When he needs inspiration, Similton need only look at himself and his siblings Levon, Willie, Sherry, Larry, Wendell and Donna. All now live successful lives. Dale says football provided him many opportunities but a sport does not define him.

"I always wanted to be much more than just a football player," Similton said recently. "Going into the Hall of Fame is a dream that I would have never expected.

"But for me, it's not all about what I have accomplished, but about the journey I took. Through the practices, all the games, all the playing in the backyard dreaming of what I might accomplish. Then through all the setbacks, I never gave up. .... If people learn anything from my story, I want it to be to always give your best, always work hard, because you never know what can happen."

("Similton to be inducted into Mars Hill Hall of Fame: Educator inspires others after journey from abandonment to success. Mars Hill induction ceremony set for Nov. 7" by Jay Edwards. Reprinted with permission from The Charlotte Observer.)

I would like to share with you a song that I wrote concerning my overall feelings on how God blessed me with this Hall of Fame moment.

PURPOSE

I was born abandoned with no voice but in

a world of freedom I found choice.

What's your purpose, it's your choice, the world is

passing and the Lamb is waiting. You can call Him Master,

King of Kings, The Lion of Judah, The Prince of Peace.

I'm servant, no I'm a King. I don't want no problems just let me be.

What's your purpose, it's your choice, the world is

passing and the Lamb is waiting. You can call Him Master,

King of Kings, The Lion of Judah, The Prince of Peace.

I'm sinner, I'm saint, my sin has been

forgiven, and I'm a new creation.

Jesus, Jesus, Jesus, He's my choice.

Jesus, Jesus, Jesus, I will never die.

Jesus, Jesus, Jesus, gives me eternal life.

I'm foreigner, I'm Prince in a world of freedom, I made my choice.

What's your purpose, it's your choice, the world is

passing and the Lamb is waiting. You can call Him Master,

King of Kings, The Lion of Judah, The Prince of Peace.

26

THE POWER OF THE THREE C'S

T
HE THREE C'S CHANGED MY LIFE FROM ONE OF FAILURE TO ONE OF
SUCCESS. I feel that sharing these words and how they continue to impact my life will open doors for others just like me to
follow their dreams. As I share them with you, consider how you can
incorporate them into your life, so that you too, will come to realize
that God has a unique plan for your life.

COURAGE
Definition: Ability to conquer fear or despair

My courage has always been in God, because in God there is perfect love and no fear. My childhood life was shattered, because I had no parents to share with me their knowledge and wisdom concerning the ways of the world. But I found courage in my faith in God and in the words my brother shared with me: "Believe in yourself even when no one else believes in you." Courage is what every person needs in order to face the many troubles in life. My sole purpose in life is to motivate and stimulate the minds of young people to believe in themselves and to show courage in the face of adversity.

CONFIDENCE
Definition: Trust, Reliance

In order to be successful you have to have confidence in yourself. For example, at Boys Town we disciplined ourselves to study for tests, as well as finish any school assignments that needed to be completed. There were always kids in the home who chose to use this time to play around or procrastinate. There were those focused on doing good concerning other people and trying to present ourselves to the public with confidence, but then there was always someone acting the fool, breaking the laws or rules, causing problems for others and wasting precious time.

Life isn't fair, but it's what you make of it and believe it to be. I'm positive that the word confidence has played a key role through my life and will continue to be a part of who I am.

CHARACTER

Definition: Distinctive quality

Character is the reflection of one's soul. Character is what will lead one to his or her destination in life. When I first came to Boys Town, my character was being shaped by my environment, role models, and education. The house parents, administrators, and others always demonstrated their love through caring attitudes, smiles, and their dependability. I never knew love had the power to break the hardness inside of me that had been created by the different elements in my childhood environment. It was tough growing up in a world with no direction. I felt anger from being rejected by my own parents, and being separated from my siblings. Feelings of inferiority chased me like a bad dream. Today, I can tell you that it was the shaping of my character that saved me from a life of criminal activity. I've come to accept who I am and what I am. I've come to terms with all of those bad dreams that had been chasing me. As I teach and coach, I reflect every day on what it means to be a positive role model. Even in my own community, I continue to live and give out of my character so that others may understand that character is a way of life and is not based on feelings.

You can reach your dreams and be successful in life by improving in the areas of courage, confidence and character in your life.

The following poem captures every second, minute, and hour that I live, because my life is not my own.

TIME

It's a new day, I can see the sunrise as I dress for work.

I'm looking in the mirror only to see the

face of man holding onto time.

It's been a long time, long, long, time.

Suddenly, there's a voice calling to me and before I realize,

I'm reminding myself of whom I am, where I'm going.

And it's been a long time, long, long, time.

I'm walking out the door with love on my mind,

preparing to save the world with hope and a prayer. Then,

I remind myself of whom I am, where I'm going.

It's been a long time, long, time.

So, here I am lost in love and saved by grace. I'm

left wondering when will change take place, where's

the perfect love, and where's paradise?

Then, I hear a voice reminding me of who I am, where I'm going.

DALE E. SIMILTON

To order additional copies of this book or to request
an appearance by the author, please contact us:

Email: DaleSimilton@gmail.com

Website: www.DaleSimilton.com

 Dale.Similton

 @DaleSimilton

 dalesimilton

Made in the USA
Columbia, SC
28 March 2018